To all people who live in fear of expressing their love, with the hope
that they may one day do so freely and openly.

Copyright

First published in 2020 by Fenton (registered as L Lambert
Holdings Ltd, company number 10807902)
in the United Kingdom.

This edition published 2020.

© Fenton and individual contributors.

The right of Fenton and individual contributors to be identified as
the author of this work has been asserted by them in accordance
with the Copyright, Design and Patents Act 1988.

All right reserved. No part of this publication may be reproduced,
transmitted or stored in a retrieval system, in any form
or by any means, without permission in writing from Fenton.

Typeset by CPI Group (UK) Ltd.

Printed in England by CPI Group (UK) Ltd.

A CIP record for this book is available from the British Library
ISBN: 9781527264137

All correspondence should be directed to Fenton.
www.fentonand.co
Fenton, 411-413 Oxford Street, London, W1C 2PE

This Book is printed using vegetable-based inks on FSC approved paper
which is derived from sustainable materials.

The printer is FSC certified ,Carbon Neutral and holds ISO 14001.

ESSAYS ON LOVE, LUST AND LOSS

CONTENTS

ORIGINS 1

EVOLUTION 62

FUTURE 126

A love letter from Fenton

2020 was heralded as the dawn of a new age; a new decade with all the hope and optimism that brings. Instead, the year so far has felt closer to the end of ages than any sort of beginning. We have seen horrific natural disasters in Australia, a proliferation of human rights abuses in the US and a global pandemic that has turned the entire world upside down.

Fenton is a new company, launched in 2019, and this has been a turbulent time to grow from infancy towards adulthood. But our mission is clear and this has helped all of us, both at work and personally, to keep a North Star in sight. Fenton exists to help people express and celebrate love. We challenge the status quo of inflated jewellery pricing and we believe that our products should provide opportunity, not exploitation, for the people who source our gemstones and craft our pieces.

In that, Fenton has a happy purpose; our team helps people express love every day, whether for themselves or for others. This is a joy in itself but we always knew we wanted to go further than this and that we had more to say.

I first started looking into the wedding jewellery industry in 2017 whilst starting to build Fenton. My impression was less than positive. I thought the existing industry painted an antiquated and conformist stereotype of love that is white-washed, heteronormative and inherently misogynistic. I kept seeing the same identikit couple across websites and adverts; he had just spent the equivalent of a down payment and she was meant to have had all her dreams come true, yet nothing of this stereotypical image of love felt real.

Having a single image of love isn't healthy. It infiltrates our subconscious and can make those who do not conform to this view of the world feel marginalised and as if their love and their emotions are somehow lesser. When we launched, I felt strongly that we could not be part of perpetuating this narrow view of the world. At Fenton we firmly believe that all love is equal and should be cherished as such.

The issue goes even deeper than this. We take it as true that the need to feel and to express love is one of the core tenets of human life and that this need is inherent to us as beings. It must then follow that the expression of love must be a basic right that applies to all people without prejudice towards race or nationality, sex or sexuality, culture or creed.

The world has changed immeasurably in the past 100 years and yet there are so many people who still live without this fundamental right. A single, but powerful example; today same-sex relations are still heavily penalised in over 60 countries with the threat of incarceration and even death. Even in more progressive nations where people have a legal right to pursue their emotions without constraint, there are still endless social factors that can stand in the way of people living and loving autonomously.

We hope you will see these essays as a coherent and intelligent argument for us all to work to ensure that the right to love freely is acknowledged and upheld. That we must all strive for greater acceptance. For the rights of the individual. For the freedom for any and all to pursue emotional fulfilment and happiness.

I started working on Notes on Love during the pandemic, reaching out to a range of talented authors, poets and people who took me out of the same four walls and shared a world of divide and struggle, hope and determination with me daily.

From one room I travelled across the world as I listened to the indomitable Payzee Mahmod, was inspired by Juno Roche's imagination and strength, was made to laugh by Flora Gill, respected Luke Day's witty subtlety, was buoyed up by Candice Brathwaite's raw energy and was touched by the heartache experienced by Alice Mann. They, and many others, have courageously offered you a naked version of their emotional selves in this collection of essays and reflections.

Every penny of the profits from the sale of Notes on Love will go to charities our contributors have chosen. We are not here to lecture or to sermonise. Instead, we want to offer a moment to dive into a range of brave and brilliant psyches who are determined to use their experiences to inspire progress and positive change. I think you will be more struck by the similarities in their stories than by the differences - I know I was.

With Love

Laura

Laura Lambert,
Founder, Fenton

'How can anyone
be against love?'

MALCOLM X

MODERN LOVE

AN INTRODUCTION BY ALEXANDRA SHULMAN

When Laura asked me to write about what she called 'modern' love, I was unsure what that might mean. What is modern love? How would we define it? Does it need definition anyway? And what on earth was I going to bring to the debate? Now the contributions are in and the range of interpretation contained within these covers is obvious, I am no clearer on the answer to those questions. But I am clear that it is a subject that continues to capture our imagination and often motivate our lives.

Love of all kinds is a subject that has no beginning nor end. It is a pillar of human existence and yet it is impossible to pin down. The ramifications of love are endless and modern love is no different to ancient love. If this collection were put together 300 years ago, the entries would of course be different, but at heart we would be talking about the same thing. Although the way we go about looking for it might change.

Last night I sat next to a writer who told me his 20 year old daughter had been having a hard time finding, what I at her age, would have thought of as love. But she felt that there was nothing to do with love about her digital hook-up experiences. She explained to him that for the past three years her and her friends should be amorous (if I can use that term) life was purely about sex. Love was not on the menu. It simply had no place in the transaction. And she was miserable, and uncertain.

It made me think, and not for the first time, how lucky I am to not to be searching for a partner in that way but more importantly it was another, of so many examples of how the search for love in our modern day is so conflicted. Now that we can have a physical relationship with anyone we chose, now that we no longer have to rely on the smallest of communities to discover love, now that we can find company of one kind or another at the swipe of a screen – the uniqueness of love seems to be even more precious.

Love, as can be seen in the variety of what has been written in this compilation, has permeable borders. And like it's counterpart hate, love is one of the most potent and powerful motivators and forces in the world. We will do anything for love. And not always wisely. In the name of love, the catchphrase goes. Love is not mild and meek. It is untameable and unpredictable. Yet it is also nurturing, warm and life-enhancing. One thing's for sure. We all yearn for it.

How many times have you been in love we ask each other? Well, now. That's a question. In love. So different from the question, how many people have you loved. I often wonder about my own answer to how many times have I been in love, that's when I'm not thinking about whether it would be nicer to live in the town or country? Or whether it's too late to learn a musical instrument? Today I think the figure is 5. But then again it might really be 3. At any rate it's a figure that bears no relation to how many people I have been involved with over the years – propelled by desire, affection, loneliness, excitement, curiosity and sometimes just proximity. And because I'm at heart a fairly hopeless romantic, when I think of love it is that heady, delicious, painful, reckless feeling of being in love that I am attracted to even though looking down from the lofty position of age I know that love, often takes a different form. Love is whatever we wish it to be – it comes from us as much, sometimes even more, than it comes from others.

Notes on Love is an anthology of different voices talking about the different aspects of love. It includes experiences and hope, advice and commentary. It's opened up the Pandora's box that love of all kinds will always be. And I hope you enjoy what's inside.

ORIGINS

one

to be e

and who ge

to be loved.

Dr Sophie Mort

'Honing Your Emotional Intelligence'

'WHAT IS LOVE?'

ALAIN DE BOTTON

Care

One way to get a sense of why love should matter so much, why it might be considered close to the meaning of life, is to look at the challenges of loneliness. Too often, we leave the topic of loneliness unmentioned: those without anyone to hold feel shame; those with someone (a background degree of) guilt. But the pains of loneliness are an unembarrassing and universal possibility. We shouldn't – on top of it all – feel lonely about being lonely. Unwittingly, loneliness gives us the most eloquent insights into why love should matter so much. There are few greater experts on the importance of love than those who are bereft of anyone to love. It is hard to know quite what all the fuss around love might be about until and unless one has, somewhere along the way, spent some bitter unwanted passages in one's own company. When we are alone, people may well strive to show us kindness; there may be invitations and touching gestures, but it will be hard to escape from a background sense of the conditionality of the interest and care on offer. We are liable to detect the limits of the availability of even the best disposed companions and sense the restrictions of the demands we can make upon them. It is often too late – or too early – to call. In bleak moments, we may suspect we could disappear off the earth and no one would much notice or care. In ordinary company, we cannot simply share whatever is passing through our minds: too much of our inner monologue is overly petty or intense, random or anxiety-laden to be of interest. Our acquaintances have an understandable expectation, which it would be unwise to disabuse them of, that their friend should be normal. We must operate with a degree of politeness too. No one finds rage or obsession, peculiarity or bitterness especially charming. We can't act up or rant. A radical editing of our true selves is the price we must pay for conviviality. We have to accept too that much of who we are won't readily be understood. Some of our deepest concerns will be met with blank incomprehension, boredom or fear. Most people won't give a damn. Our deeper thoughts will be of scant interest. We will have to subsist as pleasant but radically abbreviated paragraphs in the minds of almost everyone. All these quietly soul-destroying aspects of single life, love promises to correct. In the company of a lover, there need be almost no limits to the depths of concern, care, attention and license we are granted. We will be accepted more or less as we are; we won't be under pressure to keep proving our status. It will be possible to reveal our extreme, absurd vulnerabilities and compulsions and survive. It will be OK to have tantrums, to sing badly and to cry. We will be tolerated if we are less than charming or simply vile for a time. We will be able to wake them up at odd hours to share sorrows or excitements. Our smallest scratches will be of interest. We will be able to raise topics of awe inspiring minuteness (it won't have been like this since early childhood, the last time kindly others expended serious energy discussing whether the top button on our cardigan should be done up or left open). In the presence of the lover, evaluation will no longer be so swift and cynical. They will lavish time. As we tentatively allude to something, they will get eager and excited. They will say 'go on' when we stumble and hesitate. They will accept that it takes a lot of attention to slowly unravel the narrative of how we came to be the people we are. They won't just say 'poor you' and turn away. They will search out relevant details; they will piece together an accurate picture that does justice to our inner lives. And instead of regarding us as slightly freakish in the face of our confessions, they will kindly say 'me too.' The fragile parts of ourselves will be in safe hands with them. We will feel immense gratitude to this person who does something that we had maybe come to suspect would be impossible: know us really well and still like us. We will have escaped from that otherwise dominant, crushing sense that the only way to get people to like us is to keep most of what we are under wraps. We will start to feel like we exist. Our identity will be safe; we won't be the only guardians of our story. When the world's disinterest chills and erodes us, we will be able to return to the lover to be put back together again, reflected back to ourselves in terms that reassure and console us. Surrounded on all sides by lesser or greater varieties of coldness, we will at last know that, in the arms of one extraordinary, patient and kindly being worthy of infinite gratitude, we truly matter.

Admiration

In Plato's dialogue, The Symposium, the playwright Aristophanes suggests that the origins of love lie in a desire to complete ourselves by finding a long lost 'other half'. At the beginning of time, he ventures in playful conjecture, all human beings were hermaphrodites with double backs and flanks, four hands and four legs and two faces turned in opposite directions on the same head. These hermaphrodites were so powerful and their pride so overweening that Zeus was forced to cut them in two, into a male and female half – and from that day, each one of us has nostalgically yearned to rejoin the part from which he or she was severed. We don't need to buy into the literal story to recognise a symbolic truth: we fall in love with people who promise that they will in some way help to make us whole. At the centre of our ecstatic feelings in the early days of love, there is a gratitude at having found someone who seems so perfectly to complement our qualities and dispositions. They have (perhaps) a remarkable patience with administrative detail or an invigorating habit of rebelling against officialdom. They might have an ability to keep things in proportion and to avoid hysteria. Or it might be that they have a particularly melancholy and sensitive nature through which they keep in touch with the deeper currents of thought and feeling. We do not all fall in love with the same people because we are not all missing the same things. The aspects we find desirable in our partners speak of what we admire but do not have secure possession of in ourselves. We may be powerfully drawn to the competent person because we know how our own lives are held up by a lack of confidence and tendencies to get into a panic around bureaucratic complications. Or our love may zero in on the comedic sides of a partner because we're only too aware of our tendencies to sterile despair and cynicism. Or we are drawn to the atmosphere of thoughtful concentration of a partner because we recognise this as a relief from our overly skittish, superficial minds. This mechanism applies around physical attributes too: we may admire a smile as an indicator of a much-needed acceptance of people as they are (to counter our own troublingly punitive or acerbic attitudes) or a cheeky ironic smile may draw us in because it suggests the balancing quality to our own excessively compliant view of the world. Our personal inadequacies explain the direction of our tastes. We love at least in part in the hope of being helped and redeemed by our lovers. There is an underlying desire for education and growth. We hope to change a little in their presence, becoming – through their help – better versions of ourselves. Love contains just below the surface a hope for personal redemption: a solution to certain blocks and confusions. We shouldn't expect to get there all by ourselves. We can, in certain areas, be the pupils and they the teachers. We usually think of education as something harsh imposed upon us against our will. Love promises to educate us in a very different way. Through our lovers, our development can start in a far more welcoming and energising way: with deep excitement and desire. Aware of our lovers' qualities, we may allow ourselves some moments of rapture and undiluted enthusiasm. The excitement of love stands in contrast with our normal disappointments and scepticism about others; spotting what is wrong with a person is a familiar, quickly completed and painfully unrewarding game. Now love gives us the energy to construct and hold on to the very best story about someone. We are returned to a primal gratitude. We thrill around apparently minor details: that they have called us, that they are wearing that particular pullover, that they lean their head on their hand in a certain way, that they have a tiny scar over their left index finger or a particular habit of slightly mispronouncing a word... It isn't usual to take this kind of care over a fellow creature, to notice so many tiny touching, accomplished and poignant things in another. This is what parents, artists or a God might do. We can't necessarily continue in this vein forever, the rapture is not necessarily always entirely sane, but it is one of our noblest and most redemptive pastimes – and a kind of art all of its own – to give ourselves over to appreciating properly for a time the real complexity, beauty and virtue of another human being.

Desire

One of the more surprising and at one level perplexing aspects of love is that we don't merely wish to admire our partners; we are also powerfully drawn to want to possess them physically. The birth of love is normally signalled by what is in reality a hugely weird act; two organs otherwise used for eating and speaking are rubbed and pressed against one another with increasing force, accompanied by the secretion of saliva. A tongue normally precisely manipulated to articulate vowel sounds, or to push mashed potato or broccoli to the rear of the palate now moves forward to meet its counterpart, whose tip it might touch in repeated staccato movements. We can only start to understand the role of sexuality in love if we can accept that it is not – from a purely physical point of view – necessarily a uniquely pleasant experience in and of itself, it is not always a remarkably more enjoyable tactile feeling than having a scalp massage or eating an oyster. Yet nevertheless, sex with our lover can be one of the nicest things we ever do. The reason is that sex delivers a major psychological thrill. The pleasure we experience has its origin in an idea: that of being allowed to do a very private thing to and with another person. Another person's body is a highly protected and private zone. It would be deeply offensive to go up to a stranger and finger their cheeks or touch them between their legs. The mutual permission involved in sex is dramatic and large. We're implicitly saying to another person through our unclothing that they have been placed in a tiny, intensely policed category of people: that we have granted them an extraordinary privilege. Sexual excitement is psychological. It's not so much what our bodies happen to be doing that turns us on. It's what's happening in our brains: acceptance is at the centre of the kinds of experiences we collectively refer to as 'getting turned on.' It feels physical – the blood pumps faster, the metabolism shifts gear, the skin gets hot – but behind all this lies a very different kind of change: a sense of an end to our isolation. In general, civilisation requires us to present stringently edited versions of ourselves to others. It asks us to be cleaner, purer, more polite versions of who we might otherwise be. The demand comes at quite a high internal cost. Important sides of our character are pushed into the shadows. Humanity has long been fascinated – and immensely troubled – by the conflict between our noblest ideals and the most urgent and exciting demands of our sexual nature. In the early third century, the Christian scholar and saint, Origen, castrated himself – because he was so horrified by the gulf between the person he wanted to be (controlled, tender and patient) and the kind of person he felt his sexuality made him (obscene, lascivious and rampant). He represents the grotesque extreme of what is in fact a very normal and widespread distress. We may meet people who – unwittingly – reinforce this division. The person who loves us sexually does something properly redemptive: they stop making a distinction between the different sides of who we are. They can see that we are the same person all the time; that our gentleness or dignity in some situations isn't fake because of how we are in bed and vice versa. Through sexual love, we have the chance to solve one of the deepest, loneliest problems of human nature: how to be accepted for who we really are.

Alain is a writer of essayistic books that have been described as a 'philosophy of everyday life.' He's written on love, travel, architecture and literature. His first book, 'Essays in Love' was published when he was 23 and his books have since become bestsellers in 30 countries.

Alain de Botton

 @alaindebotton

'LOVE IS COMPOSED OF A SINGLE SOUL INHABITING TWO BODIES'

ARISTOTLE

THE BIGGER THE DIAMOND, THE BETTER THE LOVE?

SARAH ROYCE-GREENSILL

From the day we met, my future husband was in trouble. It was a coup de foudre: I fell for his UK garage MC impression; he liked that, as a 'vegetarian', I shared his 2am chicken nuggets. We were instantly inseparable. In our first year of dating, at least six of my closest friends were married or engaged, and he witnessed first-hand the hysteria that ensued - not least around the ring. One friend called me over the moon that her diamond came with the requisite certificate confirming its D-Flawless (aka eye-wateringly expensive) status. Another discovered that her boyfriend of seven years had taken an age to propose not because he wasn't sure, but because it took him three years to save up for the diamond she'd decreed must be at least two carats, or else.

Girls' dinners always reverted to the same topic: weddings, engagements and, for those without a ring on their left hand, what we'd want. Expectations were high, and my job didn't help. As a Jewellery Editor, I write about some of the most valuable gems on earth. It's a ridiculous job, one that involves trying on jewellery worth more than most people's houses: red-carpet necklaces and collarbone-grazing earrings, the odd diamond tiara, and so, so many rings. Diamonds the size of duck eggs, white, yellow and pink, so easy to slip onto my unadorned finger. My boyfriend was inundated with photos of the gems I encountered at 'work': stones that few people ever see in real life, let alone own. In hindsight, I was setting myself up for disappointment.

A side-effect of the world I work in is that my value-for-money radar is completely off-kilter. Big jewellery brands tend to describe anything below £10,000 as 'entry level' or 'affordable'. Launching a label requires immense investment, so the majority of designers are already wealthy, and privilege in the media industry is well documented. I'd meet for breakfast at Claridges or The Wolseley with jewellers, PRs and journalists whose ring fingers were weighed down by hefty identikit diamonds bought by their hedge-fund husbands, as they talked about the trials and tribulations of trying to sell their 'family flat' in Chelsea. A two-carat minimum came as standard.

As the months and years rolled by, the questions became not 'if' but 'when' my boyfriend would propose. I'd turned 30 and my unmarried status was causing consternation. When are you going to be one of us, married friends and colleagues seemed to want to know. Isn't he aware of Beyoncé's edict? If you like it then you should've put a ring on it, buddy. And my, was he only too aware.

We'd talked about getting married. He wanted to propose, he told me, but there was one huge barrier to entry: the ring. Our flourishing relationship coincided with a professional drought for my boyfriend, a self-employed headhunter. Brexit negotiations had caused business to stall, and with it my dreams of a rock. He felt under pressure to produce a ring to rival those I wrote and fantasised about. In his mind, it was the five-figure Mayfair diamond or bust, and unfortunately for me, all signs pointed to the latter.

'I'll marry you if you buy me a new Rolex,' he used to joke - one of the few in his repertoire that I found distinctly unfunny. But deep down I had to admit that he had a point. When you think about it, the investment expected to secure someone's hand in marriage isn't too dissimilar to the ancient custom of a 'bride price', paid by a groom's family to the father of his bride. In the era of gender equality, why does this bizarrely old-fashioned custom still dominate? If J-Lo's love don't cost a thing, how come the five diamond engagement rings she's received together cost a rumoured $7 million?

Of all people, I should know the answer: ingenious marketing. I'd read Edward Jay Epstein's 1982 essay in The Atlantic entitled 'Have You Ever Tried to Sell a Diamond?'. In it, he explains how the concept of diamond engagement rings has its genesis in a De Beers marketing meeting in the late 1930s. The De Beers Mining Group, which at its zenith controlled the supply of 80% of the world's rough diamonds, sought to reverse the worldwide decline in diamond prices. The answer was to convince consumers of the link between the stones and romance. "It would be crucial to inculcate...the idea that diamonds were a gift of love: the larger and finer the diamond, the greater the expression of love," writes Epstein.

Diamond rings began appearing in films and magazines, which emphasised the size and value of the stone - a practice that continues to this day (did I mention J-Lo?). N.W. Ayer, the ad agency contracted by De Beers, arranged for lecturers to visit American high schools, impressing upon young girls the inextricable link between diamonds and everlasting love. The agency advised De Beers to "Promote the diamond as one material object which can reflect, in a very personal way, a man's...success in life".

In 1947, N.W. Ayer's copywriter Fraces Gerety coined the phrase "a diamond is forever", one of the most successful advertising campaigns of all time. By 1951, 80% of US brides received a diamond engagement ring; compared to less than 20% in the 1930s. A similar campaign in Japan saw the ancient custom of betrothed couples drinking rice wine from the same wooden bowl replaced by diamond engagement rings. In 1967, less than 5% of Japanese brides wore diamonds; by 1981, that figure was 60%.

De Beers went so far as to quantify the amount a man should spend. "Two months' salary showed the future Mrs Smith what the future will be like," ran one campaign in the 1980s. "You can't look at Jane and tell me she's not worth two months' salary," it continued, concluding that, thanks to the "biggest and best diamond I could afford...Now the only thing that other men ask her is, 'When's the wedding day?'". In Japan, the rule of thumb was three months' salary. The guidelines weren't clear about the rules for the self-employed. Is he supposed to take an average of the last year's earnings? Net or gross? Should getting engaged be overseen by HMRC?

The bigger the diamond, the more successful the man and the more 'worthy' the woman, was the not-so-subliminal message. And while I was aware that this social norm had been created in a boardroom, I wasn't immune to its influence. The rocks that sparkled on the fingers of friends, colleagues and, yes, strangers on Instagram meant they were more lovable, more deserving, more worthy of devotion than I was. As Epstein put it, "a woman accepted the gift [of a diamond] as a tangible symbol of her status and achievements". My boyfriend felt guilty; like he was failing to fulfill the 'manly' duty that would allow us to move on with our life together. All because he couldn't afford a commodity whose emotional value was invented by an advertising agency.

Engagement rings are believed to have originated in ancient Egypt, when reeds were braided into a circle, the symbol of eternity, and placed on the third finger of the left hand, whose vein was thought to run directly to the heart. In ancient Rome, married women wore a gold ring in public and an iron ring at home. In Medieval times, people proposed with poesy rings: gold bands inscribed with romantic messages on the inside, like love letters worn against the skin. Rings were a symbol; a promise that had nothing to do with the four Cs. Over drinks one night with a newly married friend, I suggested that I'd like this type of proposal: after all, it was about us making a commitment to spending the rest of our lives together, not the size or price of the diamond. She looked at me as though I'd grown a second head.

Eventually, after a series of pragmatic conversations, the likes of which are never depicted in rom-coms, I managed to disabuse my beloved of the idea that us marrying was dependent on him somehow saving up a house deposit and blowing it all on a stone. Together, we found an antique ring at auction: made in the 1910s, with a simple row of old-cut diamonds, not much more than half a carat in total, but shaped by hand in an era before factories churned out cookie-cutter solitaires marketed as a shorthand for success. Its estimate was a tiny fraction of the price tags on the diamonds I encountered in swanky Bond Street salons. The relief he felt at finding a solution to the problem that had tortured him for so long was visible. It's beautiful, unique, and I love it.

My engagement ring might not elicit an audible gasp. The reaction "it's so cute!" (meaning 'small') still triggers my four-C inferiority complex. Sure, one day I would love a more show-stopping ring - find me a motoring journalist who doesn't lust after a Porsche. But, as those De Beers marketing execs know all too well, jewellery is worth far more than the intrinsic value of the materials. You can't infer from the size of a diamond how much my fiancé and I laugh, how fiercely we love, the extent to which we've got each other's back through good times and bad. My perfectly imperfect old diamonds have lived several lifetimes, and our engagement marks a new chapter in their history as well as my own. I love to think about the women who have worn them before, how they felt when they looked down at their gentle glimmer. For me, these stones are a reminder than when we say the words "for richer, for poorer," there's no shadow of a doubt that we mean it.

Sarah is the jewellery and watches editor at
The Telegraph Group and has written extensively
on all matters related to jewellery and luxury
consumption habits.

Sarah Royce-Greensill

 @srgjewel

 @sroyceyg

'LOVE IS A CANVAS FURNISHED BY NATURE AND EMBROIDERED BY IMAGINATION'

VOLTAIRE

HAPPILY EVER AFTER

HOLLY BOURNE

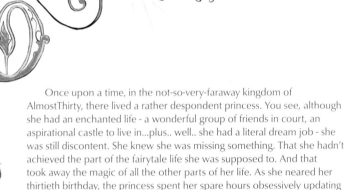

Once upon a time, in the not-so-very-faraway kingdom of AlmostThirty, there lived a rather despondent princess. You see, although she had an enchanted life - a wonderful group of friends in court, an aspirational castle to live in...plus.. well.. she had a literal dream job - she was still discontent. She knew she was missing something. That she hadn't achieved the part of the fairytale life she was supposed to. And that took away the magic of all the other parts of her life. As she neared her thirtieth birthday, the princess spent her spare hours obsessively updating herself on all the announcements from other princesses in neighbouring kingdoms. They didn't seem despondent. Plus, seemingly out of nowhere, they were all finding princes to marry and having elaborate, beautiful weddings. Had she missed the memo about a new curse or something? Did they all need to get married before thirty or they'd turn into stone?

One night, unable to sleep, the princess lurched up in her four poster bed. She knew what to do. She'd ask her magic mirror. The one she'd been given on her eighteenth birthday.

"Be careful with it," her mother had said, when she ripped off the wrapping paper. "It may be magic, but it can only grant one wish per lifetime. Use that wish wisely. Make sure it's something you really want."

And, for over a decade, the princess had resisted the call of the Magic Mirror. Had tried to solve her problems without the aid of magic. No matter how much the mirror tried to tempt her.

Every morning, when she examined her blackheads, the mirror would ask her, "Do you want to use your one wish today?"

"Not today, thanks."

"Are you sure? I could solve those blackheads?"

"Yes. I can hold on."

But, now, alone in bed, the princess was resolute, and bored of feeling left behind and jealous of other people's happiness. She couldn't wait till morning. So she pulled on her dressing gown, and padded over to the magic mirror. It was mounted on her wall - giant, gold, ornate - and it only glowed when it spoke to her.

"Magic mirror?"

The glass flickered then dimmed. "Shh. I'm sleeping."

"Magic mirror," she asked again, stepping closer and seeing herself magnified in the glass. She was getting older every day, her face slowly morphing into her mother's. Lines that stayed put when she smiled. Her youthful glow only achievable from expensive potions from the local witch, Rentinolia. "I think I want to use my wish today."

At that, the magic mirror turned the brightest gold it had ever turned. "This is very exciting."

The princess smiled. "I know."

"Are you sure? I can only grant one wish. Word it carefully."

"I'm sure."

The princess closed her eyes and pictured all the other princesses she spent so much time comparing herself to. How blissful their lives looked compared to her's. Then the princess opened them again, and said clearly, "I want to be as happy as everyone else. That's my wish."

The mirror turned the whole bedchamber to glitter, and her voice took on a new authoritarian tone. "Your wish is my command," she replied. "Follow my instructions to the letter and your wish will be granted. Firstly, in order to be as happy as everyone else, you need to find a prince to marry."

The princess sighed. She knew this was coming. She'd suspected that, despite everything else she'd achieved in her life, it wouldn't give her the happiness she saw in others.

The mirror did not offer any further guidance on what the prince should be like, so the princess was unsure what to prioritise. But, when she looked at her peers' choices, they'd all referred to their princes as 'handsome' or 'charming' so she figured that was the secret ingredient to their happier lives. After a few busy weeks of dating - kissing a few frogs, both metaphorically and literally because, well, kissing actual frogs had worked out well for her friend Princess Tiana - she'd found a willing prince.

She ran up to her bedchamber, breathless with excitement. "I've found one," she declared to the mirror. "He's both charming AND handsome. And he didn't even used to be a beast or a frog, so it's the ultimate win."

The mirror turned gold again. "Congratulations. That's the first step of the happiness spell achieved. Now, for part two. You need to get this prince to propose to you. Preferably in a really unique and romantic and public way, so you can tell everyone for the rest of your life exactly how he did it."

The princess smiled at the thought. "Of course," she said. "Yes, that makes sense. That's what I've seen the other happy people do."

So she started dropping lots of hints towards the prince about what she wanted. And then, when the hints didn't land, she started making more outright demands. Eventually, he relented, and on the night of her thirtieth birthday, at the party the kingdom had organised to celebrate all the princess's life achievements, he got down on one knee and proposed to her with a very expensive diamond ring.

"How expensive?" The mirror asked, when presented with the happy news. "It has to be at least three month's worth of his salary, otherwise the spell won't work."

"Phew, I think it was," the princess said, admiring her sparkling diamond. She did feel very happy when she looked at it. A sense of belonging to something. Though she couldn't explain what. "What next?"

The mirror turned gold again. "Now, for the spell to work, you need to publish a picture of your ring alongside the following magic words. Do you have a pen?"

The princess pulled out a quill. "Yep."

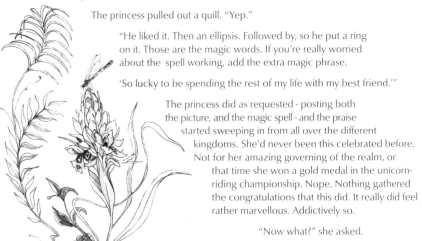

"He liked it. Then an ellipsis. Followed by, so he put a ring on it. Those are the magic words. If you're really worried about the spell working, add the extra magic phrase.

'So lucky to be spending the rest of my life with my best friend.'"

The princess did as requested - posting both the picture, and the magic spell - and the praise started sweeping in from all over the different kingdoms. She'd never been this celebrated before. Not for her amazing governing of the realm, or that time she won a gold medal in the unicorn-riding championship. Nope. Nothing gathered the congratulations that this did. It really did feel rather marvellous. Addictively so.

"Now what?" she asked.

Now you need a series of engagement portraits. To show the kingdom how in love you are, and also to practise your best angles for the big day itself."

So the princess commissioned a series of portraits to announce the engagement, which involved spending several hours staring into her prince's eyes, and a lot of nuzzling against a sunset. It all felt a bit strange and forced, but the princess overcame that by imagining how it would feel when everyone saw the portraits and told her how beautiful they both looked.

"Now what?".

"Well, you want to look completely perfect on the day, so you need to start dieting."

The princess started limiting her daily calories. Hunger became her constant companion.

"And you need a beautiful dress. One that's classic and romantic, and unique and traditional. A timeless piece that reflects the current fashion trends. Make sure you order it in a smaller size so you slim into it."

After significant stress, the princess found the perfect dress and ordered it in a smaller size. The only catch was, it was hugely expensive. As were all the other wedding preparations. The mirror had ordered her to book the most luscious castle for the ceremony, and the banquet was costing fifty gold pieces a head. Plus there were the hundreds of floral arrangements, as well as her bridesmaids dresses, the entertainment, the evening dinner, the official photographer.

"It's the only way the spell will work," the mirror promised her.

So the princess found herself emptying her royal bank account, and remortgaging her castle. "It will be worth it," she told herself. "You can't put a price on happiness."

The mirror issued further instructions which were valiantly followed. The princess organised a giant hen do away in another realm, and invited all her friends from court. Many of them seem delighted at the trip, but others were a bit sour, making comments about the expense of it. One friend said she wasn't going to come at all. And two more supposed-friends, said they could come, but couldn't afford all the activities on offer. "I'll come for some of it," one of her best friends said, "but, I'm sorry. I can't quite stretch to paying for the spinning wheel lessons. Also, I find them a bit offensive to spinsters."

The princess felt a weird rage inside her, like the friendship had been tarnished somehow. Like maybe her friend didn't love her as much as she should. Also, who was SHE to complain about money? The princess was the one BANKRUPTING herself so her friends could come to her special day, and eat her fifty-gold-pieces-a-head meal.

Another problem came up when it came to sending out invitations.

"Your father needs to walk you down the aisle," the glowing mirror told her.

The princess's mouth dropped open. "But my father has been banished from the kingdom," she protested. "He tried multiple times to curse my mother, and sometimes even me. And, the whole time he was in the kingdom, it was a dark and terrible place to live as everyone was so scared of his moods."

"If I could shrug, I would," the mirror replied. "But your father has to give you away, otherwise...."

"...the spell won't work. I know. I know."

So, with reluctance, the princess wrote to her father, inviting him. He replied instantly, thanking her for the apology she didn't remember writing, and heartily welcoming the invitation. He then put out a story on the Inter-Kingdom news about his 'appearance' at the wedding, as well as releasing never-seen-before portraits of the princess as a child.

Her mother came to her castle, sobbing and shaking, asking, "Why did you invite him? I'm terrified of him." And all the princess could do is shrug and tell the mother it was 'what's expected' and she'd try her best to ensure they don't have to sit together at the top table.

The wedding day drew closer and closer, and with it, the mirror's demands more and more incessant, until the princess was almost sick with stress. She needn't worry about dieting to fit into the magical dress, she could hardly eat anyway. Her mind was whirring with trying to perform all the requirements to get the magic to activate.

"You must arrange a perfect chart dictating where everyone should sit. You must allow for every single guest's insecurities about how far away their table is from the top table, as well as considering their past romantic histories, and their past social histories. Plus allow for there to be mingling between new groups of guests, as well as people being able to catch-up with their existing friends. If anyone is upset with the seating arrangements, the spell won't work."

"You must buy a small gift to put on the tables that is as expensive as it is totally useless - otherwise the spell won't work."

"The cake not only has to be beautiful and tasty. It must say something about your personality as a couple."

"Make sure the wedding service starts at the perfect time so everyone has enough of a day, but not too much of a day."

"Ensure that the banquet caters for carnivores, herbivores, vegans, fruitarians, lactose-intolerants, gluten-intolerants, cannibals, and pagans. Nobody is allowed to be hungry at any point."

"You must find dresses in a colour and style that suit all of your bridesmaids. They must all be happy and look beautiful. But they're not allowed to look more beautiful than you, otherwise the spell won't work."

"Your first dance at the ball needs to be choreographed perfectly and include a hilarious break-out section for people to film."

It didn't help the princess's stress levels that her fiancé wasn't really helping with anything. She tried to include him in food choices and table planning, as well as crying on him about the stress of her dad's behaviour. But he was disinterested, saying, "you were the one who wanted a big wedding,' and 'it will all be OK on the day,' while also not doing much to ensure it would actually be OK on the day.

After much fretting and worrying, soon it was the morning of her wedding. She woke early, way before her bridesmaids, and sat in front of her mirror.

"Today is the day," she whispered to the mirror.

"The happiest of your life," the mirror replied.

"Any other conditions in order for the spell to work?"

The princess couldn't help but notice that her reflection in the magic mirror was worryingly different from how she looked when she first asked about this spell. It was her wedding day. She was supposed to be glowy and content and as happy as everyone else. Instead she looked gaunt, and stressed and twitchy. Thank God the makeup artist was arriving soon, to paint a face over her own.

"Yes, just a few," the mirror replied. "Firstly, apart from your vows, you must stay silent all day. Definitely do not speak publically. That will break the spell. You are allowed to demurely chat to guests, but no speeches."

"OK, stay silent. Got it. What else?"

"There's a certain sequence of photographs you need to have captured by the end of today too. Have you got a quill, to take them down?"

The princess sighed and scrambled around for parchment.

"Right, here we go...you need a photo of the whole bridal party jumping into the air, a photo of all the prince's groomsmen holding you up horizontally, one of you both walking through a tunnel of thrown confetti, laughing and holding hands. You need line-up photos of you, him, and every different family group, and social group. You need one giant aerial shot of everyone in the wedding part, of course. And one of you throwing the bouquet, and..."

And yet, to some degree, the stress melted away once everyone woke up and started fussing over her. The princess had never been fussed over like this her entire life. All her friends told her how gorgeous she was, and then her parents actually managed to be civil to each other and too tell her how gorgeous she was.

She walked down the aisle, finding every single person's eyes following her, like she was the most important person in the realm, and they all told her how gorgeous she was afterwards.

She looked into the eyes of her prince, and he told her she was gorgeous, and she truly believed, in that moment, as they shared their vows, that this was the truest, most beautiful love.

The day passed crazily fast, especially as the princess had so many parts of the spell to complete. It was a shame that everyone she loved most in the world was there, and yet she hardly got more than a minute's chat with any of them, before she had to drag the prince away for a particular photograph. She sat demurely and silently through the banquet and speeches, and twirled gorgeously at the nighttime disco, pulling off the perfect transformation from serene virginal bride, to fun-loving party bride.

With a blink, it was over. Guests left, leaving their table favours behind, mumbling their thank-yous, saying it was a beautiful wedding, and then complaining they were hungry once they'd climbed into their horse and carriages. The newly-minted couple retired to the honeymoon turret, and once she'd performed the final act of what was expected of her that day, he fell asleep, leaving her married, and alone with her thoughts.

She smiled for a while. Remembering all the good bits. She looked at all the messages she was being sent, saying what a great day it was and how gorgeous she looked, and she felt even happier.

For a moment or two.

But, as the night went on, too buzzed to sleep, she waited for the blissful happiness to arrive. The euphoria. The feeling of utter contentment she'd been promised. She lay next to her new husband, staring at his face, and she felt love... yes, she did, but not an overwhelming amount. It was just him and her now, she guessed. This. Them. Together. With no wedding to plan anymore.

Shouldn't she feel happier?

Then, an update pinged in from a princess in a neighbouring kingdom. Anxiously, she checked what the big news was - finding this other princess had just announced her own engagement and the biggest wedding the realm had ever seen. Everyone was ecstatic about the news. The congratulations came in thick and fast. It was like they'd forgotten it was HER wedding day. She realised, sadly, her day was over now. It was old news. Fading. Blurring into the smudge of every other princess's wedding, which was just like hers.

She tried to wake her prince for comfort. Nudging him, whispering his name. But he only batted her off and turned over on his silken pillow, before letting out a loud, continuous snore.

She didn't feel happy.

In fact, she felt a bit empty and sad.

She thought she'd followed the spell to the letter, but maybe she'd got some of it wrong?

Unable to handle it, she threw on her robe and padded through the castle to her old bedroom, where the magic mirror was waiting, dormant.

She knocked on the glass to wake it.

"What do you want?" the mirror asked, grumpily. "It's 2am."

"The spell," the princess said, a tear rolling down her face. "It didn't work. What did I do wrong?"

The mirror sighed wearily. "It did work. Well done. You did everything right. Don't worry. I granted your wish, just as you asked."

More tears spilled from the princess's eyes. "That can't be right," she said. "Because I don't feel truly happy!"

The mirror sighed again, like it was readying itself for sleep again. "My darling," she said. "You didn't ask to be truly happy, you only asked to be as happy as everyone else... Which, you are."

The mirror turned to pure glass, never to glow gold ever again.

And the princess lived as happily ever after as everyone else does.

The End

Holly is a Times best selling author who writes for teens and adults. Her works include 'Am I Normal Yet' and 'How Do You Like Me Now' as well as her debut adult novel, 'Pretending'.

Holly Bourne

📷 *@hollybourneya*

🐦 *@holly_bourneYA*

DRESSES WITH A PERSONALITY: BRIDALS

GIANLUCA LONGO

I am often asked if a dress can be a statement. 'Dresses show the personality of who wears them' would be my immediate answer. Bold colours, audacious prints, sexy shapes, outrageous cuts can definitely make a statement dress: who dares, wins.

When it comes to wedding dresses, these can be even more than a statement. Wedding dresses happen to reveal fascinating personal insights into the lifestyle, and tastes, of their owners. Some dresses make bolder statements about identity and personality than others; a strong-minded woman and a statement dress definitely make for a unique bride.

On the subject, one of my very first fashion memories is Norman Hartnell's creation for socialite Margaret Whigham (later to become the scandalous Duchess of Argyll). She married the dashing Charles Sweeney at the Brompton Oratory in 1933 in a Morticia Addams-style dress, with stars embroidered all over. It made such an impression to the general public that the traffic in Knightsbridge was blocked for three hours!

Since that day, many more wedding dresses - and the women wearing them - have made even more memorable impressions.

How can we forget the pink gingham shirtwaist dress that Brigitte Bardot wore at her second wedding in 1959? Or the canary yellow chiffon number that the uber glamorous Elizabeth Taylor wore to marry her fifth husband Richard Burton in 1964? And Cilla Black's red velvet mini dress? Actually wearing a non-white wedding dress is in itself a statement. Colours have different meanings when it comes to that. Red stands for strong emotions, infatuation, energy. Pink is more about child-like personality, innocence, good health. I wonder if any of that was behind Gwen Stefani's choice for that ombre pink gown, designed for her by John Galliano at Dior in 2002... Blue suggests stability, security and lifelong loyalty. Black instead is often looked upon as an eerie colour - an odd but definitely bold choice for a bride. Denoting power, sophistication and formality it was the right colour for Lydia Pang's ruffled number. 'I wanted to be comfortable, larger than life, gothic, but feminine and modern' she commented about the look.

Regardless of history, trends and wealth, most people will still agree that the symbolism of the white wedding dress is purity.

That doesn't mean it can't be notorious.

Mini skirt, felt hat and knee-highs, all in white, hit the headlines for Yoko Ono's big day with John Lennon. It was 1969. Bianca Jagger's low-cut white skirt suit was by no means conventional, and left little to the imagination: it was Sex and Rock and Roll.

A wedding dress can make the woman. In the case of Margaux Hemingway, her sweetly ruffled lace one immortalised the actress as a timeless beauty icon.

The super short goofy meets body-con dress that Rita Wilson wore to marry Tom Hanks in 1988, screamed fun from every stitch. She is often remembered for her choice, which remains impactful to this day. Of the same genre is the tea-length dress, in tulle, designed by Chanel, that Kiera Knightly sported to tie the knot. She loved it very much, and was seen in it again and again at various red carpet events and parties.

Arriving at the wedding by bicycle can be a statement too. And you wish the dress would allow you to do so. It surely did for Solange Knowles, in her Stephan Rolland Haute Couture jumpsuit.

More than unexpected is to read the brides' favourite poem on her veil, as it was chosen by Greta Bellamacina. Her country style dress was perfect in the backdrop of the wilderness of an Exeter farm where the nuptials happened to be.

The location of a wedding can also be of inspiration for a statement dress. Poppy Delevingne asked her favourite fashion designer and best friend Peter Dundas to make the biggest, loveliest and most romantic wedding dress that could fit with the atmosphere of Marrakech's Beldi Country Club. Well, the lace embroidered roses on her dress matched perfectly with the roses in the garden of the resort. She walked through it at sunset looking dreamy, and married her beloved James Cook.

Gianluca is the Style Editor for both British Vogue and Cabana Magazine. In his longstanding career as a fashion and lifestyle journalist he has written broadly on fashion, interiors and lifestyle and regularly hosts talks on fashion and design.

Gianluca Longo

 @gianlucalongogg

 @gianlucalongogg

HONING YOUR EMOTIONAL INTELLIGENCE

DR SOPHIE MORT

I am not afraid to admit that I have spent a large portion of my life focussed on all of the wrong things.

It started in my teens. A time when I believed that in order to have a good life (read: be accepted and worthy in the eyes of others), I needed to be better. Smarter, faster, hotter, richer. Someone who impressed others and owned all the stuff.

I believed that if I could be all of these things, I would be happy and I would be accepted.

Dr Sophie Mort is a registered clinical psychologist, life coach and yoga teacher. She also works as a guide on mental health app, Happy Not Perfect.

Dr Sophie Mort

 @_drsoph

These beliefs and the constant comparisons I made to my peers and the people on TV and in the magazines, partly drove me to work harder in my quest for all-round-perfection. But mainly, they drove me to exhaustion. I spent a significant amount of time criticising and berating myself. I felt anxious, miserable and almost constantly like a failure.

To the outside world I probably looked like I was doing pretty well, as I hid these feelings behind a smile and a "me? I'm great! Yep, totally fine! Thanks for asking". Oh, and that was the other thing: I thought the only acceptable emotion was happiness and anything else was to be avoided, pushed away the moment it arose.

I genuinely thought I was doing the right thing. I didn't question whether it was making me miserable, or in fact, whether it was helping me to achieve what I ultimately wanted in life: that age-old goal of feeling accepted.

This is not the story of a troubled teen, or a particularly anxious adult.

While I thought I was the only one struggling with this in school, I now as an adult and a clinical psychologist - who spends most days talking to people about their psychological pain - know that this is actually an experience that most people can relate to.

Humans are hardwired for connection. Being in groups kept our species alive for millennia. That is part of the reason we are so driven to be part of something, to be valued, loved, cared for, truly seen and heard. When we are connected and accepted, we feel safe. Scratch that, we feel amazing.

A deep connection is fostered through vulnerability, empathy and deep human understanding. Not a shiny exterior, straight A's or money.

How could I, and so many others, have gotten so caught up on the wrong things?

There are millions of reasons but I will give you two to start:

1) We are surrounded by adverts that tell us perfection is not just attainable, it is necessary. Think of the images you see each day. Images of people who look a certain way, and have all the things. The implicit message being: Look like this, buy this, and you will be loved. You will be happy.

Advertising relies on our insecurity. If we felt content in who we were we wouldn't buy nearly as much.

2) We are not taught about our psychology growing up. We are not taught about our emotions and how we can understand them and manage them when they arise.

So, we come out into this world and instead of learning how to connect with ourselves and other humans on a true and deep level, we get distracted. We get tricked into the rat race of do better, be better, impress us all.

What can we do about this?

I believe that one of the main tasks of growing up is unlearning the ideas fed into us about who gets to be enough and who gets to be loved. Let's replace these ideas with the knowledge that we are all worthy of this and that we are better when we are connected, and when we surround ourselves with people who are not afraid to be flawed.

And then, we need to work on our emotional intelligence.

Emotional intelligence (EI) was described by its founding fathers, Salovey and Mayer, as "the ability to monitor one's own and others' feelings and emotions, to discriminate among them and to use this information to guide one's thinking and actions."

If we work on our EI we can recognise that all emotions have a purpose and that we can learn from them. We can stop pushing emotions away and instead recognise them and remain present. Then take time to consider what may be causing them and choose how we wish to respond.

We may even decide to harness the power of our emotions to promote our thinking and productivity. For example, certain 'negative' emotions, such as anger, have been shown to fuel creativity, as long as the emotion is not yet overwhelming.

Once we understand our own emotions, we can even start putting ourselves in other people's shoes. We can understand how that person may feel and then choose to act in ways that improve the situation and support them, if that is what we wish to do.

It means we can read what might be happening under the surface of someone's experience, even when they say, like I did as a teenager, that everything is "ok".

How do we improve our emotional intelligence?

Emotional intelligence is something we have to work on and it takes time. It is not a quick fix. It is not being happy and motivated all the time, which is another unattainable goal. It is about being able to be where we are and at the same time remain present and able to choose what we want from life.

Here are the first steps:

1. Learn a new set of rules about emotions:

Emotions are normal - all of them. None of them are bad or good, even though some feel better than others. Emotions start in the body and are generally fleeting, if we allow them to be present and don't push them away or fear them. We all vary in how strongly we feel our emotions depending on our genetics and our life experiences - this is normal too.

2. Increase your ability to recognise your emotions, your triggers and your patterns:

Most of us are stuck in our heads only noticing our emotions when they are strong and maybe screaming at us. You can learn more about your triggers and emotional responses through journaling, body scans and/or mindfulness meditation.

Mindfulness meditation allows us to create space and a little bit of time after a new emotion arises and before we set off into our autopilot ways of responding. For a quick mindfulness practice you can try right now, try the STOP technique: Multiple times per day say to yourself Stop, then Take 3 deep breaths, Observe what is happening in your body and decide how you want to Proceed.

3. Learn solid coping skills, including breathing exercises and emotion labelling:

Grounding techniques and breathing exercises will keep your body in the present moment and soothe your stress responses. They need daily practice if you want them to be genuinely helpful during times of stress. Another skill for your tool box is labelling: Neuroscience has shown us a quick way to tame our emotions is to label them. It's easy: When you next feel a strong emotion arise, turn your attention towards it and decide on a label for it. When you do this the activity in your brain shifts. The activity in the amygdala (the emotion centre of your brain) dampens, allowing the part of your brain responsible for being in the present moment, problem solving and decision making to come back online.

4. Start mirroring other people's behaviours:

Look at your friends, or even just people in the street. Copy their posture, gestures and anything else you see them doing while they are doing it. If they can see you, make this subtle - we don't want it to be weird! As you copy them you will get a sense of what it feels like to be the other person. You will get a sense of their intention and the emotions behind their actions. Equally, as your friends see you subtly mirroring their behaviour it will signal to them that you are attuned to their experiences.

Like I said, this isn't a quick fix. This is just the start. It is work. And like all self work, it can be slow and challenging. However, it is work that will teach you about yourself and give you better ways to look after yourself and others when emotional turmoil arises. It will help keep you on track with your wants and needs, making you less susceptible to feelings of failure and other anxieties drummed up in our everyday interactions. It will help you truly connect with other human beings.

Instead of trying to be 'smarter, faster, hotter, richer', let's focus on being connected - to our emotions and to each other.

LOVE IN THE LYRICS
'SOMETHING' – GEORGE HARRISON

ORSON FRY

When George Harrison began tapping away at a tune in an empty Abbey Road studio in 1968, he could be forgiven for thinking the melody coming from the piano wasn't his. It came to him so easily, he suspected he must have lifted it from another song, so he put it on ice for six months. "That is too easy. It sounds so simple. It must be something," he thought, "but it wasn't." In January of '69 the Beatles returned to the studio and during a rehearsal session for what would become the Let it Be album, George showed the song to the others and 'Something' was born.

George walked into the studio on January 28, 1969 with most of its parts figured out. But lyrically he was struggling to find a fitting simile to end the first line. You can hear this exchange in the recorded tapes of that now famous

session. "What could it be Paul?" George asks. "Just say what comes into your head each time," John cuts in, "Attracts me like a cauliflower! Until you get the word."

George settles into the song and the band follows, throwing out lyric ideas as they play. "Screwdriver?" teases John, before having a go at the beautiful descending line at the end of the verse. By the end of the take they still haven't finished the line. "Attracts me like a pommygranit," George jokes, a little exasperated.

Harrison would take the song away and finish it on his own, thankfully overcoming the fruit and vegetable predicament to find an original simile to end that first line. But it's no wonder he struggled. Throughout the song Harrison is getting at the indescribable - that something in the way she moves, in the way she smiles, in her style, in the way she knows, and suggestively, in the things she shows him. He's trying to put words to something without any, namely the very essence of the woman he loves. There is tension as the song dramatically changes key and Harrison, with searing vocals, addresses the question of whether his love will grow; and a complete and swelling honesty in his answer—a frank admission of his love and its bounds. As if words are not enough, Harrison gives us what's perhaps the most beautiful and note-for-note perfect guitar solo of all time. Music is not to be written about and music writing is generally all guff, but this song stands apart from other love songs. There are no vows, no sentimental overtures, just pure feeling.

In a 1969 interview, Harrison was asked what had inspired 'Something' and he answered "Maybe Pattie, probably"— referring to his then wife Pattie Boyd, who would later leave him for his friend Eric Clapton. But when asked the same question years later, he distanced himself from the idea that the song was written about one woman, and instead pointed to the Hindu god Krishna and a more universal idea of love as its possible inspirations.

Seven months and thirty-nine studio takes after that first rehearsal session, 'Something' was completed and chosen to become the single on Abbey Road. It was the first and only time a Harrison composition graced the A-side of a Beatles single, becoming the song by which he managed to break the Lennon-McCartney songwriting hegemony. After only 'Yesterday,' it became the most covered Beatles song of all time, with everyone from James Brown, to Smokey Robinson and Sinatra covering it. As Ol' Blue Eyes himself once introduced it: "It's one of the best love songs I believe to be written in fifty or a hundred years... and it never says I Love You."

Orson is a writer and musician living in London. He is one half of the band 'Some People'.

Orson Fry

 @orsonfry

A MODEST PROPOSAL: PLAN YOUR MARRIAGE, NOT YOUR WEDDING

KATE WILLS

It's very easy to lose sight of the bigger picture when you're heading for a wedding. Tiny details take on huge significance. The inconsequential feels of utmost importance. If you know a couple who are about to get married, ask them if they've done their table plan yet. It'll be like you've told them they'll need to perform open-heart surgery on each other while wearing a blindfold. I personally spent many frenzied hours hand-pressing 163 wild flowers as if my life depended on it, not just my guests' place settings. In the excitement and stress that is the build-up to your Big Day, what often gets lost is why you're doing it in the first place. I should know. Within a year of my wedding, my husband and I were getting divorced.

Why did I want to get married in the first place? I've spent a lot of time thinking about that lately - even more time than I spent painstakingly sandwiching daisies between Hilary Mantel books. I wanted to get married to feel more grown-up – there's something annoyingly child-like about referring to your 'boyfriend' when you're well into your thirties. I wanted to make some sort of commitment – we'd bought a flat already, and I wasn't ready for a baby. I desperately wanted the female rites-of-passage that are shopping for 'The Dress' and having a hen do. I felt like everyone else was. And, yes, I was in love. Who's to say what the right reasons are for getting married. But given how things turned out for me, I can see how not all of mine were coming from the best place.

Initially, I told myself I wasn't going to get caught up in all the usual wedding fuss. There'd be no sugared almonds or choreographed dances for me, thanks very much. There would be no proposal video or 'I said yes' announcement on social media. I was more bride-chiller than bride-zilla. In fact, I proposed to him on Hampstead Heath with a ring made out of a twig. There was absolutely no way we were going to spend all of our savings on a single day. But I soon found out that it's hard to push back against the pressures of a wedding industry worth £10 billion in the UK.

Simply wanting to celebrate with all your friends and family - let alone finding a venue that could fit and feed them all in London - felt impossible to do without spending an eye-watering amount. Before I even really realised it, I was booking choirs and coffee vans and forking out more than I make in a month on a dress I knew I'd only wear once. This didn't feel unusual. In fact, it felt necessary. In my head, our wedding was a reflection of ourselves – or to be more accurate, myself. This wasn't just a party; this was a demonstration of how stylish, how creative, and how unique I was. Therefore every decision felt fraught with intensity. The costs kept spiralling.

Friends have told me that they too lost all sense of control when it came to photobooths and oyster bars and pre-wedding personal training regimes. I'm certainly not the first bride-to-be to get carried away. And irritatingly, among heterosexual couples, the wedding planning does always seem to fall on the woman. Perhaps it's because so many nuptial traditions are rooted in misogyny – your dad 'giving you away', a white dress to symbolise virginity, and so on – that we barely recognise how deeply sexist it is to expect women to sort every detail. Every venue-owner, caterer and celebrant we saw spoke only to me, as if my partner was merely a vaguely-interested party. Planning the wedding made me feel like I had a second full-time job, one involving even more spreadsheets than my actual career. Which isn't to presume that men are disinterested. A friend confided in me that her husband felt really left out of their wedding planning, and would've loved to have had more say.

I quickly discovered that if you add the word 'wedding' to even the most ordinary items – cakes, dresses, flowers – then you can also add a zero to the price. Which is probably why the "average" UK wedding, that's Mr and Mrs Normal not Mariah Carey, costs over £30,000 (more than the average annual salary).

In the US, where the wedding industry is worth a mind-blowing $53 billion, they're starting to see a backlash to the wedding madness. I've heard reports of couples planning 'Shadow Weddings', where they dress in their slobbiest clothes, voice their worst neuroses and acknowledge each other's most irritating traits - a pretty extreme but possibly necessary reaction to how overblown many ceremonies can get.

It's hard to say why so many weddings have become so removed from reality. Partly, it's the intensity of social media. When you know yours will be tagged and viewed and – let's be honest – judged by many more people than you invited, it goes from Big Day to Big Deal. Many people have pointed to extravagant celebrity weddings as the reason for this trend – if Kim and Kanye's multi-country affair cost a reported $12million, surely you can splash out on a food truck or a flower arch? Whatever the cause, as more and more of us up the stakes with our special days, a hugely-anticipated, giddily-heightened spectacle becomes the standard many of us feel we have to aspire to.

And this matters. Because as I became increasingly focused on all things Wedding, I lost sight of what I really should've been investing time and energy on: my relationship. I spent so long compiling playlists, registering for presents and choosing poetry readings, but no time at all thinking about what our life

I had lost sight of the fact that the marriage is the main event, not the day itself, no matter how good the DJ at the after-party is

together would look like. Any doubts I had about getting married I blamed on wedding jitters. All the fights we had in the run up were put down to the stress of wed-min. We had been together 12 years so of course he was 'The One'. Although things hadn't always been perfect, I felt like getting married was the step we needed to bring us closer. Some people have a 'band-aid baby'; I can see now that I had a 'band-aid big day'.

Looking back, I wish we'd spent just a fraction of our wedding budget on some pre-marriage counselling. Within many religions, 'marriage preparation classes' are part of the process for many couples. It certainly makes sense to tackle issues before you tie the knot, or make sure that your foundation is solid before problems arise. But I was too swept up in the wedding-planning juggernaut. I was in a bubble. I had lost sight of the fact that the marriage is the main event, not the day itself, no matter how good the DJ at the after-party is.

I can honestly say that our wedding – which took place in a multi-story carpark - was the best wedding I've ever been to. I still look back on it with love and wonder, which isn't always the case. Some friends felt so caught up in the stress of achieving nuptial perfection that they couldn't even enjoy their own wedding: one burst into tears because she couldn't stop thinking about the fact the caterer had brought the wrong dessert; another was so fixated on it being "The Best Day of Her Life™" that she found it impossible to relax and have fun.

Despite what happened next for me and my now ex-husband, our wedding day was a celebration of us and the 12 years we'd spent together. Sadly, we are proof that a great wedding doesn't always equal a great marriage. In fact, a study from Emory University in the US found that the more expensive the wedding, the more likely a couple are to split.

Many people are surprised to hear this, but I think of my marriage as a success. We spent over a decade together and we are still friends. I'd wanted to get married as a way of stepping into adulthood, and I can assure you that nothing makes you feel more grown-up than getting divorced.

I have a new partner now and I wouldn't rule out getting married again. There's a hopefulness about the gesture that I love, and rituals are important. But I think next time, I'd elope. That way I could ensure that it really was just about us and our future. I have a tendency to get a bit carried away, you see.

Kate is a journalist and writes for The Times, The Guardian, VOGUE, ES Magazine, ELLE, Grazia, The Telegraph, SUITCASE and Red, as well as being a columnist for Fabulous Magazine.

Kate Wills

 @katewillswrites

 @katewills

ICONIC
COUPLES

Cleopatra & Mark Antony 41BC

Arguably one of the most iconic couples in history, the illustrious love affair between Cleopatra VIII, queen of Egypt, and Mark Antony, a Roman general has been well documented throughout history. As the story goes, Antony, who was placed in charge of Rome's Eastern territories, summoned Cleopatra to the city of Tarsus, to answer charges laid against her for helping enemies of the Roman Empire.

Cleopatra for her powers of seduction and political brilliance and orchestrated an arrival so magnificent that Antony was besotted with her from the instant he saw her sailing down the Cydnus River dressed as Venus the Roman god of love. It was clearly an overwhelming spectacle as he immediately followed her back to Egypt with a promise to protect her crown and country.

The following year, called for by his comrades, Antony returned to Rome, and in a gesture of loyalty to his nation married Octavia, the half-sister of his fellow ruler Octavian. Back in Egypt, Cleopatra gave birth to Antony's twins, Alexander Helios and Cleopatra Selene, and continued to rule over the land until the two were reunited years later. Antony's return to Egypt greatly dismayed his former ally Octavian. As tensions boiled over between the two men, a war between their nations soon ignited and in 31 B.C. the Battle of Actium was fought, and lost, by Antony at sea.

Following the battle, Cleopatra retreated to her mausoleum for safety. Antony, having been falsely told that she had died in anguish, stabbed himself with his own sword, meeting his death in dramatic fashion. Cleopatra later returned to her chamber and committed suicide alongside two of her female servants, bringing to a close this epic tale of tragic love.

Oscar Wilde & Lord Alfred Douglas 1891

Oscar Wilde and Lord Alfred Douglas met via a mutual friend in 1891 and, although Wilde was married with two sons, they began a secret relationship. Their affair was tempestuous and heated with frequent fights, breakups and reconciliations. Wilde famously used his great literary talents to write a series of stirring love letters to Douglas, addressing him by his childhood nickname 'Boise';

'it is a marvel that those red rose-leaf lips of yours should be made no less for the madness of music and song than for the madness of kissing. Your slim gilt soul walks between passion and poetry. I know Hyacinthus, whom Apollo loved so madly, was you in Greek days.'

Douglas's father, the Marquess of Queensberry, began to suspect that the relationship was romantic in nature and set out to destroy Wilde and salvage his son's reputation. The Marquess left a note at Wilde's club, openly accusing him of being a 'sodomite' which started an open feud between the two men. This accusation eventually led to the 1895 trials in which Wilde was publicly prosecuted for homosexuality and convicted to two years in jail. During the trial one of Douglas's poems, Two Loves, was quoted which contains the infamous line often mistakenly attributed to Wilde; 'I am the Love that dare not speak its name'.

Douglas was exiled to the continent and although they briefly reconciled in Naples after Wilde's release, the reunion was to prove brief as Wilde died in 1900. Following his death, Douglas was married and had one son. He died many years later in 1945 and his relationship with Wilde remains an enduring source of fascination for biographers and historians to this day.

Gerda Gottlieb, a Danish artist who specialised in fashion illustration and erotic paintings of women, met and fell in love with her fellow artist Einar Wegenar (later Lili Elbe) at the Royal Danish Academy of Fine Arts, when they were just 19 and 22 respectively. They married in 1904, as Gottlieb's profile as an artist was beginning to rise. As her interest in the concepts of gender and identity grew, Gerda asked her husband to sit in as the model for a female portrait one day when her usual model failed to arrive.Thus began the start of their artist-muse relationship, with Wegenar fast becoming his wife's favourite model and assuming the alter ego of Lili.

It was through these sittings that it became clear that Einar, identified as male-to-female transgender. In 1912, the couple moved to Paris, where they could live openly as a same-sex couple. Consumed by her body dysmorphia, Lili sought out gender reassignment surgery which, in 1930, was still highly experimental. She underwent four risky procedures to transform her body, becoming one of the very first documented recipients of gender reassignment surgery.

Given Gottlieb's rising success and popularity, the King of Denmark, Christian X, soon became aware of her marriage to Elbe - by then legally a woman - and annulled their union under Danish law in 1930. The two decided to part ways amicably to avoid legal trouble.

Lili went on to get engaged to an old friend, and planned a final surgery in an attempt to create a working uterus and fulfill her dream of becoming a mother. Sadly Lili passed away from heart paralysis whilst in recovery from her final surgery; she was just 48 years old.

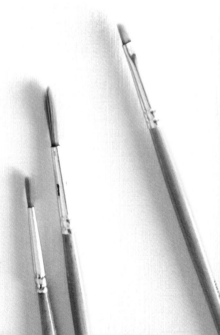

June 12th marks the unofficial holiday of Loving Day, which celebrates and honours Richard and Mildred Loving's triumph in over-turning anti-miscegenation laws. After an almost decade-long saga which spanned the couple's blossoming romance, marriage, subsequent arrest and exile, the ban on racial intermarriage was abolished in a Supreme Court victory in 1967.

Mildred Jeter, who was of African and Native American descent, met Richard, a white man, through her older siblings when they were both teenagers. Despite not initially clicking, the pair gradually developed a friendship that eventually blossomed into a romantic relationship. When Mildred fell pregnant at 18, the two decided to marry. Matrimonial unions between interracial couples were illegal in their home state of Virginia, so the couple eloped to Washington D.C. in June 1958. Several weeks later, the police stormed their home whilst they slept and arrested them both, charging them with "cohabiting as man and wife, against the peace and dignity of the Commonwealth".

Given the choice of serving a 12-month sentence in prison or being exiled from Virginia for 25 years, the Lovings moved to Washington D.C., where they raised their family. Inspired by the civil rights movement of the time and eager to return home, Mildred reached out to the American Civil Liberties Union for help overturning their exile. Over the course of four years, the ACLU took Loving v. Virginia from the Virginia county circuit court all the way to the Supreme Court, which unanimously ruled miscegenation laws as unconstitutional nationwide.

In the Court's opinion, Chief Justice Earl Warren stated that marriage was a basic civil right and that to deny this right on the basis of race would be "directly subversive of the principle of equality at the heart of the Fourteenth Amendment".

The Lovings returned to Virginia, where they lived openly as a legally married couple until Richard's untimely death in a 1975 car accident, at the age of 41. Mildred followed him in 2008, having never remarried.

Surrounded as I am now by wonderful children and grandchildren, not a day goes by that I don't think of Richard and our love, our right to marry, and how much it meant to me to have that freedom to marry the person precious to me, even if others thought he was the 'wrong kind of person' for me to marry.

MILDRED LOVING

'SEDUCTION AND SCANDAL IN JANE AUSTEN'S ENGLAND'

CLEMENT KNOX

Most British newlyweds will be familiar with the reading of the banns: the public announcement of the couple's intention to marry made in church on at least three Sundays in the months preceding the wedding. The practice might seem now to be a minor bureaucratic hassle—a relic of the distant past. In fact, it was the product of some of the most urgent debates surrounding sex, consent, and seduction that preoccupied eighteenth century England.

Prior to 1753, marriages were technically legal upon the exchange of vows between the bride and groom. This didn't have to happen in a church or in any formal setting: the words just had to be uttered and the couple were married. The law distinguished between a promise to marry (per verba de futuro) and a declaration of marriage (per verba de praesenti) but provided legal protections for both. For instance, if a man promised to marry a woman and reneged on the offer leaving her high and dry (and often pregnant, too), then the woman could sue him under Breach of Promise to marry. This freewheeling system might now seem rather informal and more than a little anarchic. At the time it was very popular. Young men and women keen to escape the control and censure of their parents ran away to marriage shops (in London these were concentrated around

Fleet Prison in Farringdon) to get hitched quickly and discreetly. Its popularity was such that even after the practice was erased in 1753 it persisted in Scotland (where under the Act of Union of 1707 a distinct family law was preserved), creating the practice of English couples eloping to Gretna Green, just as Lydia Bennet attempts to do in Pride and Prejudice.

What changed then in 1753? That was the year that Lord Hardwicke's Marriage Act passed through Parliament. The bill's full name — 'An Act for the Better Preventing of Clandestine Marriage' — gave a flavour of what its supporters aimed to prohibit. For the ruling class this unregulated system of marriage was a challenge to their authority. Specifically, it threatened their estates. Every wealthy family lived in terror of their heir or heiress getting informally married to an actress or a conman and frittering away their family's property. There was no real provision for divorce in the eighteenth century so once someone was married that marriage could not be undone. What God had joined together, no man could put asunder. This was exactly the argument that bill's supporters foregrounded. The Attorney General Sir Dudley Ryder praised the bill as 'designed for putting an end to an evil which has been long and grievously complained of, an evil by which many of our best families have often suffered.' Namely, 'for guarding against the many artful contrivances set on foot to seduce young gentlemen and ladies of fortune, and to draw them into ... infamous marriages.'

The Marriage Act was also framed as a device to specifically protect women from devious male seducers. Incredibly, the ruse it was designed to prevent was the custom of paying an imposter posing as a priest to officiate at the 'wedding'. In Samuel Richardson's Pamela, perhaps the single best-selling novel of the eighteenth century, the titular heroine is warned in an anonymous letter of a plan afoot to seduce her by this means. 'The squire is absolutely determined to ruin you,' she is told, 'he will pretend great love and kindness to you, and that he will marry you. You may expect a parson, for this purpose, in a few days; but it is a sly artful fellow, of a broken attorney, that he has hired to personate a minister.' There is evidence that this practice really did exist. In his memoir, composed shortly before his execution at Tyburn in 1730, the legendary London outlaw James Dalton admitted that he had taken a 'Gentleman's Daughter' to St Clement's Church on the Strand and 'married' her with 'my Acquaintance the Procurer performing the Part of the Father'. Afterwards, bride and groom got wildly drunk and went by coach to the Bell Inn in West Smithfield. The next morning Dalton, wicked fellow that he was, crept away from the marital bed and vanished into the East End.

The Marriage Act put an end to all this. It required a public ceremony conducted in a church or chapel according to the Book of Common Prayer, preceded by the readings of the banns or the purchase of a licence. This was the only form of legal marriage now recognized in England, although the law carved out exceptions for Jews, Quakers, and members of the Royal Family. The net effect was to bring marriage firmly back under the control of fathers and priests. It was also a blow to unmarried women. The old system had, in its own idiosyncratic way, provided for the protection of young women who made youthful indiscretions. By granting legal status to informal marriages and promises of informal marriage, it provided a way of protecting the moral, social, and financial standing of women who were otherwise at risk of being left pregnant and penniless should they be seduced and abandoned. The Marriage Act removed those protections. This was an argument made at the time. 'As to the fair sex,' one of the bill's detractors declared, 'it would prove a snare for entrapping many of them to their ruin [...] A young woman is but too apt by nature to trust to the honour of the man she loves, and to admit him to her bed upon a solemn promise to marry her. Surely the moral obligation is as binding as if they had been actually married: but you are by this Bill to declare it null and void.'

Of course, under the new bill that 'solemn promise' had no legal bearing. This illuminates why in Pride and Prejudice the whole Bennet family gets so wrapped up in the drama of Lydia's flight from Brighton with Wickham. Had she made it to Gretna Green and married under Scottish law then she would have certain legal protections. But once the couple veers off course and heads to London then they know that Lydia is now totally at Wickham's mercy. The taboo's against extramarital sex—especially for the respectable middle classes—had been reinforced by the 1753 Marriage Act and so Mr Collins's letter in which he declares that 'the death of your daughter would have been a blessing in comparison of [her seduction]' was a fair reflection of bourgeois attitudes in Austen's England. Of course, Mr Darcy saves the day and the reader can join in the relief of the Bennet family once Wickham and Lydia are brought safely to the altar and are married—banns and all—according to the law.

Clement Knox studied Modern History at the University of Oxford and is the author of 'Strange Antics: A History of Seduction'.

Clement Knox

 @prince_clembo

 @ClementKnox2

LOVE IN THE LYRICS
'MAKE YOU FEEL MY LOVE' –
BOB DYLAN

ORSON FRY

As a massive Dylan fan, I really struggled to pick my favourite of his love songs. So I picked a handful of them, and played each one to my girlfriend across the kitchen table. 'I Threw It All Away?' Too sad. 'Girl From the North Country?' No, not for a bridal book, darling. Ah, what about 'My love, she speaks like silence.' No! dreary! So I hit her with the big three. 'Lay Lady Lady?' Yup, that's good. 'Forever Young?' - she looked on the verge of tears. And then I played 'Make You Feel My Love,' and the floodgates just opened.

'Make You Feel My Love' is from Dylan's 1997 album 'Time Out of Mind' which proved a huge commercial and critical success for Dylan after a seven year album drought. It went on to win three Grammys in '98, including Album of the Year, and received glowing reviews from critics across the board, with only one notable exception. Rolling Stone was unimpressed with track no. 9, 'Make You Feel My Love,' and panned it as "a spare ballad undermined by greeting-card lyrics." Well, as the poet Rilke once said, "Nothing touches a work of art so little as words of criticism," and how true in this case his words would sound.

Ever since Billy Joel released it as a bonus track for his 97' Greatest Hits album, it's been covered by over 450 artists, from Adele, who had huge chart success with it in the UK, to Bryan Ferry and Neil Diamond—even Jeremy Irons tried his hand. It's stamped its mark on contemporary pop culture in a way no other Dylan song has. And it's precisely because of this wide-ranging appeal, and its apparent melodic and lyrical straightforwardness, that people are often surprised to find out who wrote it. They think it's Billy Joel or Adele. And that is his genius! That the man behind such sophisticated love songs as 'Love Minus Zero,' 'Sad Eyed Lady of the Lowlands,' or 'Tanged Up In Blue,' can also pen a ballad that one day Ed Sheeran would introduce to his Glastonbury audience as his favourite song.

What touches me about the song is that here is Dylan, the elder statesman who's seen it all, seen worlds rise and fall, pledging his unconditional devotion to one person and we believe him. Rich in imagery without being distracting, laden with sentiment without being gushy—only he can do that. I remember my Mum saying that listening to Bob got her through her divorce to my father. If you believe his voice, his words can heal.

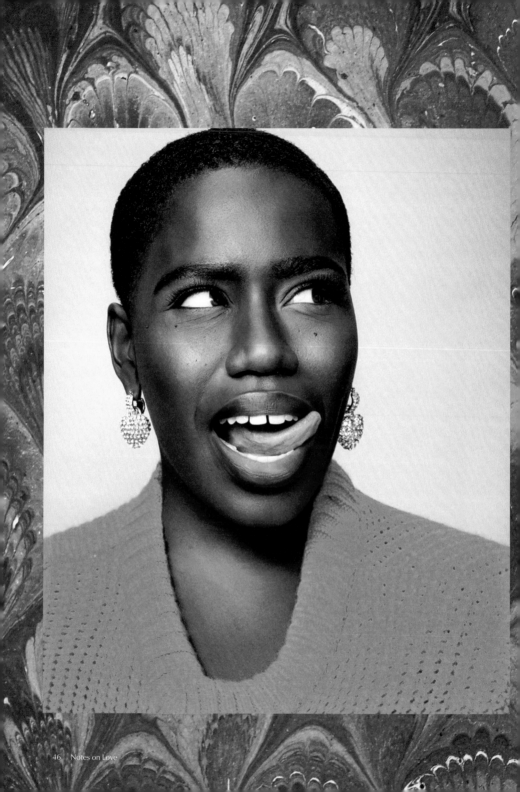

CHOOSING TO COMMIT

CANDICE BRATHWAITE

My husband loved me before I even knew him - at least that's how he will tell the love story to our children, I'm sure. See we are the fruition of romance laying down with technology. Unbeknownst to me, Papa B as I call him had begun to follow me on Twitter. I was a fast girl, living a fast life. Think all the combined characters of Sex and The City just with more melanin and a rambunctious south London attitude. And like most of my peers at that time, I was documenting every move in all aspects of my life on Twitter. This includes details about all the boys I was dating at the time.

When I finally paid attention to yet another DM from this guy - who would often remark on me sharing my running stats from my Nike+ app or try to kick start a conversation by also saying he loved eating at a restaurant I mentioned that I could already no longer remember the name of - I was just about coming out of one of the worst relationships in all of my twenties. When I say coming out of it, I mean I was metaphorically moving on my stomach, trying to make my way through the debris and bramble that only a love war could create. That's how bad that relationship was.

He was a breath of fresh air, the intake of which showed that there were no airs and graces about him. He was a born-again self-starter who had already tussled with the trappings which come alongside trying to prove yourself as a man to the world, instead of your household. He had himself come out of a long-term relationship with the only thing worth proving himself to, a daughter.

I tried to ignore his clear advances, which would lead to us going on a date. Since leaving that terrible relationship, I had taken to being a rolling stone, adamant that it was my duty to break men's hearts before they broke mine because I was tired of the former. It was still summer, and Brixton, where we were finally due to meet, was pulsating with the warm buzz of people drinking outdoors and laughing with friends. I saw him before he saw me and it took all I had to not run back towards the main road, change my number and delete all my social media.

Also he was so different to anyone I had even ever considered dating. I'd watched romcoms enough time's to know that there could be some joy in that - going down the love lane less travelled - but I wasn't Meg Ryan so I couldn't be bothered.

So unbothered I was that by the time I did cave and go on a date with him, I was very prepared, expectant almost to dislike him in the flesh. Sure, everything looks rosy from behind social media tinted spectacles but in reality, it could have been far from. But as it turned out I wasn't to be so lucky. He was very sweet. Too sweet in fact. Looking back, it's clear that I had been in such terrible relationships that my need to be stimulated by someone as chaotic and as untethered as myself was a major red flag. His eyes were hypnotic. Where God had given me two pronounced almonds, He had merely given him small slits which often made it hard for me to ascertain where he was looking. If he was really pleased, they would grow slightly bigger but only just and you would have to watch him long enough, so you didn't miss the magic happen.

He lived alone and didn't have much in the way of friends. I felt kinship in that. Although outwardly I had a vast friendship circle, I did often wonder how many of them were actually lifelong companions. If I were to drink too much in a social setting, I would often skulk off and amuse myself with thoughts of the future that included very few of them. But I wasn't confident enough to actually be alone. He was. Said confidence shone out of him like the needy bulb in a lighthouse.

He was very romantic. As our relationship developed, he wasted no time in calling me his girlfriend and while I couldn't yet return the favour, we were spending every hour with each other. Weeks rolled into months and soon it was a year. It was shortly after that year that I fell pregnant with our daughter Esmé. She was like a serious full stop which came rolling into my life. All of a sudden I had to think about being connected to this man, for all eternity.

As I'm penning this during the necessary lockdown due to COVID-19, I have to set the scene and let you know that it is with mind-numbing boredom that I decided to hop onto one of those websites that let you know all about your family tree. I'm estranged from most family members on both parents' sides so crafting it is taking far longer than I would like but what has been interesting to note is how much of a woman's life is underwritten and then overrode by her giving herself to a man. Maiden names mean so little when they in fact still carry the weight of patriarchy. Even in black and white, these women don't ever seem to be able to fully come into their own until they decide to get married or have children with a man.

Whilst most women have been dreaming about their big day since they could play celebrant to their Barbies and Kens', I had been consumed with crafting a life that only ever had me as the starring role. No extras, no long-term commitments and definitely no children.

But here I was, in love and pregnant. I hadn't planned for this level of...stability. I was supposed to be the rich auntie who yacht-hopped and could never be reached by phone but would randomly send £500 to my nieces and nephews. Deciding to have children and commit to a long-term relationship was one of the scariest agreements I've ever signed off on. Of course, there is comfort to knowing that you are loveable despite your flaws but in admitting that, it's also important to share that such stability does come with a side of wonder.

What if I had? What if I hadn't?

As a new friend so eloquently put it 'No new dick...ever.' And yes, there is that too. Our current relationship abides by the old fashioned version of monogamy and it's just us two looking at each other, day in and day out. When that's become a normal you didn't plan for, you find yourself quietly but constantly asserting your independence because it's important to remind the person you're with that you still have an idea about who you are and what you like, outside of your union. Especially if you are a woman.

This isn't to completely erase the wonderful things he not only has carried into my life but also helped me reveal about myself. He has walked with me in the darkest trenches and has opened the shutters to allow the sunlight to bathe my face when I didn't have the energy to do it for myself. We have had a few health scares during our eight-year relationship and each time I'm reminded that there is no one else I would rather do battle with. More to the point, he has shown me that real love shouldn't be a battle or war. True love shouldn't feel like a brawl. It should be the connection between people that allows them to strategize a master plan that will help them fight to see another day.

Candice is a Sunday Times Bestselling author and the Founder of Make Motherhood Diverse. Her debut work 'I Am Not Your Baby Mother' was published in 2020 to critical acclaim and she continues to tirelessly promote the cause of black mothers and families.

Candice Brathwaite

 @candicebrathwaite

 @CandiceAbodenn

MARRIAGE
TRADITIONS
FROM AROUND
THE WORLD

Spain

The old traditional Spanish wedding custom of brides wearing black was born out of the Catholic faith. Brides wore a black wedding dress with a black lace veil, known as a 'mantilla,' to walk down the aisle as a symbol of their devotion and commitment "till death do us part".

Greece

In Greece there is a tradition where all the names of the single women attending the celebration are written on the bottom of the bride's shoes. It is believed that those that have worn off by the end of the festivities will be the next to be married.

India

In India, it's customary for the bride-to-be to spend hours being painstakingly decorated with mehndi paint, a substance derived from the powdered dry leaves of the henna plant. The result is a beautiful and intricate work of art that lasts roughly two weeks on the skin. An added bonus, the mehndi is full of medicinal properties that are thought to help the bride stay calm and stress-free on her wedding day.

Nigeria

Nigerian brides have the lucky option to change outfits multiple times during a celebration. One popular choice is a traditional Igbo outfit that is made up of a blouse and tightly wrapped skirt, colourful bead necklaces and a head wrapper. In a traditional ceremony called 'Igba Nkwu' the bride will carry a glass of wine from her father to her husband who hides amongst the guests while she searches for him. When they have both sipped from the cup they are officially wed.

Cuba

In Cuba, it's tradition for every man who dances with the bride on her wedding day to pin money to her dress as a wedding gift for the newlyweds, with these generous contributions usually used by the happy couple to offset both their wedding and honeymoon expenses.

Native American

Native American tribes traditionally include a specially designed wedding vase as a part of the marriage ceremony. The vase has two spouts as a symbol of two lives becoming one and the couple separately takes a sip of water from the vase before simultaneously drinking from its double spout. Each wedding vase is reflective of each tribe's artistic techniques and historical cultural folklore, making the wedding vase unique to each couple.

Democratic Republic of Congo

In the DRC there is a tradition called 'La Presentation' where, if a man is not ready to propose or cannot yet afford to marry, but still wants to show the bride and her family that his intentions are serious then he can arrange a ceremony where he presents gifts and formally secures parental approval for the relationship.

Ethiopia

In Ethiopia the bride and groom traditionally pay homage to elder members of their family in a ceremony called 'kissing the knee'. As the happy couple enter the wedding venue they pause to kiss the feet of their parents, grandparents or great-grandparents and in turn are given blessings for happiness and health.

Lebanon

At a Lebanese wedding the guests will need to be on their toes in case the bride and groom decide to partake in the tradition of stamping on their guests' feet for good luck. The pressure can then turn back on the groom who may have to prove his strength and masculinity by lifting a large stone dish, the 'jurn el kibbeh' in front of the bride's parents.

China

In ancient times, a bride's family would hire a so-called 'good luck' woman to prepare her for the wedding and look after her as she travelled from her home to her groom's in a festively adorned bridal sedan chair. As she was carried to the chair a sister or an attendant would shield her with red parasols whilst another would toss rice at the chair as a symbol of health and prosperity. Long associated with success, loyalty, honor, fertility and love, the colour red plays an important role in Chinese weddings.

Hawaii

Nature plays a large role in traditional Hawaiian wedding ceremonies. A key part of Hawaiian culture is the chants that were originally sung at the weddings of Hawaiian royalty, one of the most important of these being the 'Kumulipo', also known as the Creation Chant which connects a couple with nature and the sea. A couple may also wrap a piece of lava rock in a ti leaf and leave it as an offering to symbolise and bless their union.

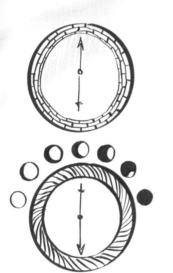

Thailand

In Thai tradition the day of the wedding is chosen by consulting a monk or an astrologer who will review the couples birthdays, dates of key life moments and the lunar calendar to find the most auspicious date. Luck will also be woven into the ceremony via the number nine which is seen as lucky. Nine monks will start the day by blessing the couple and they will serve a selection of nine dishes for each course at their reception.

Japan

On her wedding day, a Japanese bride celebrating with a traditional Shinto ceremony wears white as a symbol of her purity from head to toe, including her makeup, kimono, and a hood called a "tsunokakushi". The colour white signifies her maiden status, whilst the hood, which is worn throughout the ceremony, has long been symbolic of veiling the bride's so-called 'horns of jealousy' and her resolve to become a gentle, loving wife.

POETRY

SAPPHO, 620 BC

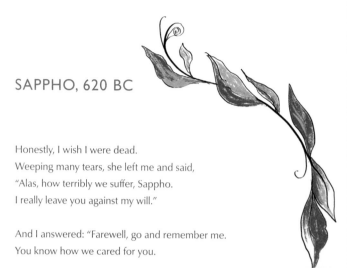

Honestly, I wish I were dead.
Weeping many tears, she left me and said,
"Alas, how terribly we suffer, Sappho.
I really leave you against my will."

And I answered: "Farewell, go and remember me.
You know how we cared for you.

If not, I would remind you
...of our wonderful times.

For by my side you put on
many wreaths of roses
and garlands of flowers
around your soft neck.

And with precious and royal perfume
you anointed yourself.

On soft beds you satisfied your passion.

And there was no dance,
no holy place
from which we were absent."

CHORUS OF THE WOMEN FROM THE 'THESMOPHORIAZUSAE'

ARISTOPHANES, 411 BC

They're always abusing the women,
  As a terrible plague to men;
They say we're the root of all evil,
  And repeat it again and again,
Of war, and quarrels, and bloodshed,
  All mischief, be what it may.
And pray, then, why do you marry us,
  If we're all the plagues you say?
And why do you take such care of us,
  And keep us so safe at home,
And are never easy a moment
  If ever we chance to roam?
When you ought to be thanking Heaven
  That your plague is out of the way,
You all keep fussing and fretting,
  "Where is my Plague to-day?"
If a Plague peeps out of the window,
  Up go the eyes of men;
If she hides, then they all keep staring
  Until she looks out again.

OH HEAVEN!

ANON HAN DYNASTY POET, 206BC-220AD

I want to be your love for ever and ever,
Without break or decay.
When the hills are all flat,
The rivers are all dry.
When it thunders in winter,
When it snows in summer
When heaven and earth mingle,
Not till then will I part from you.

RUMI, 1207-1273

This is love: to fly toward a secret sky,
to cause a hundred veils to fall each moment.
First, to let go of live.
In the end, to take a step without feet;
to regard this world as invisible,
and to disregard what appears to be the self.
Heart, I said, what a gift it has been
to enter this circle of lovers,
to see beyond seeing itself,
to reach and feel within the breast.

THE SONG OF TROILUS FROM TRIOLUS AND CRESSIDA

GEOFFREY CHAUCER, 1380'S

If no love is, O God, what feele I so?
And if love is, what thing and which is he?
If love be good, from whennes cometh my wo?
If it be wikke, a wonder thinketh me,
Whan every torment and adversitee
That cometh of him may to me savory thinke,
For ay thurste I, the more that ich drinke.

And if that at myn owene lust I brenne,
From whennes cometh my wailing and my plainte?
If harm agree me, wherto plaine I thenne?
I noot, ne why unwery that I fainte.
O quikke deeth, O sweete harm so quaintitee,
But if that I consente that it be?

And if that I consente, I wrongfully
Complaine: ywis, thus possed to and fro
All stereless within a boot am I
Amidde the see, bitwixen windes two,
That in contrarye stonden everemo.
Allas, what is this wonder maladye?
For hoot of cold, for cold of hoot I die.

SONNET V

PETRARCH, 1304-1374

O wandering steps! O vague and busy dreams!
O changeless memory! O fierce desire!
O passion strong! heart weak with its own fire;
O eyes of mine! not eyes, but living streams;
O laurel boughs! whose lovely garland seems
The sole reward that glory's deeds require!
O haunted life! delusion sweet and dire,
That all my days from slothful rest redeems;
O beauteous face! where Love has treasured well
His whip and spur, the sluggish heart to move
At his least will; nor can it find relief.
O souls of love and passion! if ye dwell
Yet on this earth, and ye, great Shades of Love!
Linger, and see my passion and my grief.

O passi sparsi, o pensier vaghi e pronti,
O tenace memoria, o fero ardore,
O possente desire, o debil core,
O occhi miei, occhi non già, ma fonti;
O fronde, onor delle famose fronti,
O sola insegna al gemino valore;
O faticosa vita, o dolce errore,
Che mi fate ir cercando piagge e monti;
O bel viso, ov'Amor insieme pose
Gli sproni e 'l fren, ond'e' mi punge e volve
Com'a lui piace, e calcitrar non vale;
O anime gentili ed amorose,
S'alcuna ha 'l mondo; e voi nude ombre e polve;
Deh restate a veder qual è 'l mio male.

AGAINST BLAME
OF WOMEN

GERALD FITZGERALD,
4TH EARL OF DESMOND, 1398

Speak not ill of womankind,
'Tis no wisdom if you do.
You that fault in women find,
I would not be praised of you.

Sweetly speaking, witty, clear,
Tribe most lovely to my mind,
Blame of such I hate to hear.
Speak not ill of womankind.

Bloody treason, murderous act,
Not by women were designed,
Bells o'erthrown nor churches sacked,
Speak not ill of womankind.

Bishop, King upon his throne,
Primate skilled to loose and bind,
Sprung of women every one!
Speak not ill of womankind.

For a brave young fellow long
Hearts of women oft have pined.
Who would dare their love to wrong?
Speak not ill of womankind.

Paunchy greybeards never more
Hope to please a woman's mind.
Poor young chieftains they adore!
Speak not ill of womankind.

WHOSO LIST TO HUNT, I KNOW WHERE IS A HIND

SIR THOMAS WYATT, 1503-1542

Whoso list to hunt, I know where is an hind,
But as for me, hélas, I may no more.
The vain travail hath wearied me so sore,
I am of them that farthest cometh behind.
Yet may I by no means my wearied mind
Draw from the deer, but as she fleeth afore
Fainting I follow. I leave off therefore,
Sithens in a net I seek to hold the wind.
Who list her hunt, I put him out of doubt,
As well as I may spend his time in vain.
And graven with diamonds in letters plain
There is written, her fair neck round about:
Noli me tangere, for Caesar's I am,
And wild for to hold, though I seem tame.

REPUBLIQUE FRANÇAISE
0.65
H. MATISSE

PARIS
POSTES
GARE ST. LAZARE

'Courage knows no gender. Love knows no limit. Sexuality is not a choice, it's a spectrum, and that's what I love most about life'

Luke Day, 'I Don't Search, I Find'

MOMENTS OF NOTE IN THE HISTORY OF LOVE

To this day, the conversation around love, marriage and relationships continues to evolve and remains a prevalent part of our society and political agenda as people across the world fight for greater acceptance for all genders, races and sexualities.

c. 9000 BC - The Ain Sakhri lovers are sculpted. These are the oldest known representations of two people engaging in sexual intercourse.

c. 7000 BC - Amongst Neolithic and Bronze Age descriptions of gender one writer describes 'a third sex' which can be either a person without defining sexual characteristics or a person with a mixture of male and female sexual characteristics.

c. 630 BC - Aristocrats in Crete adopt formal, lifelong sexual relationships between men and boys that were not dissimilar to heterosexual marriages.

390 AD - Nonnus's 'Dionysiaca' is the last known piece of Western literature for nearly 1,000 years to celebrate homosexual passion.

529 - The Christian emperor Justinian I blames homosexuals for issues such as 'famines, earthquakes and pestilences'.

533 - The Byzantine Empire declares that it will 'punish with death, not only those who violate the marriages of others, but also those who dare to commit vile acts of lust with men.'

1140 - The Decretum Gratiani is published which declares that 'In conjugal debt the woman has equal rights to the man and the man to the woman so that neither a wife may make a vow of abstinence without the consent of her husband, nor the husband without the consent of his wife'.

1533 - Henry VIII finalises his divorce from Catherine of Aragon in order to marry Anne Boleyn. In doing so he breaks with the Roman Catholic Church and forms the Church of England.

1549 - Thomas Cranmer publishes the Book of Common Prayer which contains the first version of marriage vows as we know them today.

1664 - Maryland passes the first British colonial law banning marriage between slave owners and slaves and also declaring that any white women who had married black men should become enslaved.

1722 - Peter the Great enacts a ban against forced marriages in Russia.

1780 - Pennsylvania repeals its 1725 law against interracial marriage in a bid to promote increasingly equal status between its citizens.

1791 - France adopts a new penal code that no longer crimilises sodomy, thereby becoming the first Western country in the world to legalise homosexuality between two consenting adults.

1836 - The Marriage Act allows for non-religious ceremonies to be held in registry offices.

1857 - The Matrimonial Causes Act allows ordinary people who do not possess great wealth to seek a divorce.

1861 - The UK death penalty for sex between two consenting men is revoked.

1870 - The Married Women's Property Act allows married women to become the legal owners of and inherit property in their own right.

1917 - With the Russian Revolution, Bolshevik leaders declare that 'homosexual and heterosexual relationships are treated exactly the same by law.'

1931 - Dora Richter becomes the first known transgender woman to attempt a complete sex change from a man to a woman in Berlin.

1967 - The US Supreme court declares that State bans on interracial marriage are in violation of the US Constitution.

1967 - The UK Sexual Offenses Act decriminalises homosexual acts between two men over the age of 21 in private.

1969 - The Stonewall protests take place in New York City, seeking recognition for same-sex rights.

1969 - The UK Divorce Reform Act allows couples to legally separate without having to prove 'fault'.

1978 - The Rainbow Flag is first used as a symbol of gay pride.

1996 - In the 'White vs. White' case, a landmark judgement acknowledges the contribution of a 'homemaker' and rules that assets should be split fairly.

2000 - Alabama becomes the last state to officially legalise interracial marriage.

2013 - The Same-Sex Marriage Act is passed in the UK, allowing same-sex couples to marry legally.

2014 - The UK passes an act that makes it a criminal offence to force someone to marry, either in the UK or abroad.

2020 - The first same sex marriage is held in Costa Rica, the first Central American country to equalise marriage legislation. There are now a total of 29 countries in the world that have legalised same-sex marriage.

WHY YOU SHOULDN'T LOSE YOUR VIRGINITY

FLORA GILL

I was nineteen the first time I had sex. I think because I'm a sex writer people assume I must have mastered the art early. Like all those prodigy violinists who pick an instrument before they can talk and quickly become experts, I too should have been getting my 10,000 hours in as soon as puberty hit. But in fact, I was relatively late to the sexual party.

That's not to say I was innocently staying away from the opposite sex. As a teenager, I snogged everything with a pulse. Going out dancing or to a party was a failure if I didn't aggressively tongue at least two other human beings. At one event, I remember frenching my 5th man of the night for a cigarette. I let his smoked tongue roll around my mouth as I waited impatiently to trade the organ for a menthol.

It would have been easy to have sex during school. As a teenage girl, it's never really hard. I went to a mixed boarding school surrounded by horny boys, but I didn't pop my cherry there, mainly because the act felt too big to partake my peers, too exposing. I couldn't stand the idea of them whispering in chemistry, sharing the sordid details of the night they took my virginity.

Instead, I had sex during my gap year with a boy who didn't know it was my first time and who I would never have to see again. He bought me a bucket of jungle juice cocktail and we grinded in a bar by the sea. He picked an eyelash off my face and asked if he could have my wish - the wish was about me anyway he said. Then he asked if I'd come back to his hotel. Sleeping with him was a calculated decision. I didn't want to go to university a 'virgin', so I pounced on a boy in Laos less than 24 hours after my best friend had done the same thing with another victim.

A week later, he ghosted me.

Flash-forward 10 years and the boy, now a man, found me on Instagram and slid into my DMs. 'You write for GQ?' he wrote, 'you might be the most accomplished person I've ever slept with'.

Like any reasonable millennial I took to twitter to canvas responses, first setting the scene and explaining this was the boy I'd lost my virginity to a decade earlier. Suggested replies included, 'who are you?', 'well you're the least accomplished person I've ever slept with' and 'I have a 10 year old who would like to meet you', but one of the answers that caught my eye wasn't a suggestion at all but a woman calling me out for my choice of words. 'I don't think you should be saying you 'LOST' your virginity'.

If I'm honest, I'd never really stopped to think about the wording around 'virginity', but as soon as I saw it highlighted, I realised its absurdity and the way it had impacted my decisions. I was reminded of those years I'd spent panicking about not wanting to 'lose it' to someone I knew, but not wanting to go to university until it was gone. I didn't want to be a virgin and didn't want to lose my virginity - an impossible feat.

Let's look at the facts of virginity. Firstly, there is no medical or biological distinction between being a virgin and not being one. For men this is obvious. They jizz from the moment they're able to: first into hands, then maybe socks, then for posh wanks into empty condoms, but the first time they do it into a woman's vagina, they're not physiologically changed any more than when they did it in a mouth or against their grandmother's hand towel. For women, some people point to the hymen, but you can break that from a number of activities such as sport and you can even have sex with your hymen remaining intact.

So virginity is just the term we've given to the state before you have sex. But there's no logic behind a magic moment occurring after this particular act. There's no reason for 'p' entering 'v' to be any different to 'p' in 'm' or 'a' or between your 'ts' or accidentally hitting your 'e' and needing to be washed out with drops to avoid a nasty case of conjunctivitis. The line is there because society decided it should be. The phrase 'any hole but God's hole' comes to mind and I remember the girls and guys at school who were having anal sex between classes to keep their precious virginities intact. Just imagine God looking down on all the virgin girls getting their back doors broken in and smoking cocks like lollipops, thinking 'yes, that's the way to do it'.

And what is sex anyway? What do the parameters by which we've defined virginity mean for those who aren't heterosexual. Do gay men and women not have sex? A number of my male friends have never slept with a woman, some of them have never put their penis into another person. But to call these men 'virgins' is laughable. Their sex lives make my life look like a nunnery and it's literally my job to get laid.

And all of this doesn't even touch on the phrasing around the act, the most problematic of which is the connection with 'loss'. When we talk about 'losing', we imply that the latter version is something lesser, that a part of us is gone and can't be returned, that you are irredeemably changed. We also tend to say 'he took her virginity', or vice versa, as if virginity is a prized possession it's valuable to barter from someone.

Before contraception and other scientific breakthroughs, virginity was needed to ensure that a woman's pregnancy could be attributed to the correct man. But now that we have means for preventing pregnancies and for knowing whom the father is, the distinction isn't needed.

The language we use matters. There are lots of 'firsts' that can have meaning: the first time you explore your body, the first time you fall in love, the first night you spend with someone, but the amount these matter and how they shape us shouldn't be determined by anyone else. We shouldn't pretend there's a meaningless point at which you transform and we shouldn't act like anything is lost. Sex can be incredible and rather than lose something you can gain an awful lot. But by continuing to use heteronormative, outdated language we cheapen our experiences and our worth. A penis is not important enough to metamorphose you from one state to another, neither is a vagina. You should have sex whenever you're ready to and not feel the weight of the words impacting your decision. Virginity is a social construct that needs to be left in the past. We have outgrown it. So, let's continue having sex but stop losing our virginities.

Flora is a journalist who has written on a broad range of topics spanning from Brexit to sex tips for GQ, Sunday Times Style Magazine, Spectator, Evening Standard, The Sunday Times Magazine, Radio Times and Tatler.

Flora Gill

 @floraegill

 @FloraEGill

Nude on grey with white blanket & blue wall

Hester Finch, c/o Partnership Editions

RELATIONSHIPS IN BLACK AND WHITE

VICK HOPE

Is love ever truly colourblind?
Should it be?

"You don't see a blackbird mating with a dove," my parents were told when they announced they were planning to start a family together.

Newcastle, the late 80s, and their relationship was met with resistance on both sides, from both communities, their own blood; Nigerian and English, black and white. They were advised not to "breed", the blatant bigotry of which was countenanced with the perhaps well-intentioned "we worry about whether your half-caste children will be strong enough to cope with the prejudice they will have to face".

"Intermarriage is one of the most provocative words in the English language"
Clotye Murdock Larsson, Marriage Across The Color Line

We coped pretty well. Of course we did. And moreover, others coped with us pretty well. You only have to look at every other cereal/sofa/banking TV advert to know that interracial families have become accepted and normalised. Attitudes towards mixed-race people have changed drastically. We are now more than half a century beyond the landmark ruling of Loving v. Virginia, the Supreme Court case that struck down state laws banning interracial marriage. The Immorality and Prohibition of Mixed Marriages Amendment Act in South Africa in 1985 was one of the early legislative steps towards the end of apartheid. In the UK, mixed-race people are the fastest-growing ethnic group (according to censuses in 2001 and 2011, with the next set for March 2021), as Royal baby Archie Harrison Mountbatten-Windsor "joins the ranks of those second-generation mixed-race kids who challenge our very perceptions of ethnicity and black identity," writes Matthew Ryder in his article on 'The changing face of mixed-race Britain'. In fact, you could say that the changing face of mixed-race Britain is quite simply just the face of Britain, in glorious technicolour. Or at least, it seems, that's where we're headed.

"Love is blind despite the world's attempt to give it eyes"
Mashona Dhliwayo

However, just because we see interracial relationships doesn't mean that we don't see race. It doesn't mean we've put our differences aside and melded into one, happy, united, totally unprejudiced human race. As long as there is still deep-rooted institutionalised racism in the world – and there is, Lord, there is – it is reductive to claim race as a purely social construct to not only be transcended, but disregarded. We are shaped by our cultural upbringings, and what a fucking glorious thing that can be! It's taken me almost three decades to feel this way, as I'll discuss in due course, but I certainly see my dual heritage to be a strong, vivid, sometimes tumultuous, constantly evolving part of my identity; something to embrace rather than disregard. Something to love and – hopefully, by someone – be loved.

But exactly what role does race play in the theatre of love? Whether we're swiping on an app, catching eyes across a crowded room or arriving at that dizzying moment in which you realise you've fallen for your soul's counterpart, what does their background (or yours) have to do with it? Which racial fetishes might underpin our 'type', and equally can tacit prejudices explain those 'massive turn-offs'? How does culture impact who we connect with, and who we can live with? We always say relationships are not black and white, but perhaps, in some ways, they are...?

Let's take, for example, online dating. Here, courtship is coloured in distinctly different hues for different users. According to the study 'Black/White Dating Online: Interracial Courtship In The 21st Century', black people are ten times more likely to contact white people on dating apps than vice versa; while in 2014 OKCupid found that black women and Asian men were rated substantially lower than other ethnic groups on its site, with white men the most sought after demographic. Tinder's algorithm, which reportedly ranks attractiveness based on previous swipes (as posited in Safiya Umoja Noble's 'Algorithms of Oppression: How search engines reinforce racism') surely reinforces society-specific ideals of beauty, which remain prone to racial bias. And perhaps most pertinently, a 2018 study by researchers at Cornell University shows that 17 of the 25 highest grossing dating apps allow users to filter others by ethnicity.

You may not see 'No Blacks, No Irish, No Dogs' signs anymore in real life, but you sure as hell can tick a box to fend off entire ethnic groups if you don't think you fancy them; if they're just not your type.

These straightforward categories segmenting desire along search terms such as height, hair colour, weight, gender and race reflect the keyword-heavy approach of online porn, and all the stereotypes that are tangled up in fetishisation. Of course, it would be better to quantify desire via "world view, or sense of humour...slippery notions that might well underpin a true connection, but are often hard to define," writes Thomas McMullan in his article questioning 'Are the algorithms powering dating apps racially biased?' - and so we are left with these "un-imaginative algorithms, which are a problem". The word 'match' – so small and seemingly innocuous – in fact hides a heap of judgements, where the line between 'preference' and 'prejudice' is undeniably – dare I say, sinisterly – blurred.

"The greatest lie ever told about love is that it sets you free"
Zadie Smith, On Beauty

Long before the internet though, dating was – and still is – often bound by racial and economic/class factors: your neighbourhood, your work, your place of worship, the food you enjoy, the bars you frequent, and the families and friends you socialise with. I for one, for better or for worse, definitely have had a 'type' based on my background. Without a doubt, race has played into that.

Growing up in Newcastle in the 90s, my mum was one of very few black people I knew: there were only three at my school, a handful of kids of Chinese, Indian and Pakistani heritage, and not a single other mixed-race child other than my brothers. It's difficult to be tangibly attracted to something that barely exists in your world. And apart from briefly lusting over Tyson Beckford on Make Me A

Supermodel, it's even more difficult to actually forge any kind of relationship with them. I fancied skinny, preppy, white boys with messy brown hair, because they looked like the guys in the bands I liked, and crucially, because there were tons of them about.

Onto university: Cambridge, 2007-2011. Much of the same, to be honest. But this time they were book-smarter, and posher. I fell deeply in love with one of them, and for six years we had the time of our young, carefree lives before growing apart, as adolescent sweethearts so often do. My second, and only other, long-term relationship was once again with a skinny, preppy, white boy with messy brown hair, from a relatively privileged background. We met in my new hometown of London, at a time when an increasingly diverse social circle was having a formative impact on my sense of belonging and identity. I'd started learning more about my background and educating myself about my history. It didn't occur to me at the time, but looking back I think this triggered a resentment towards him that festered in me, bristling into arguments about not understanding one another, and our eventual break-up. This was a turning point.

"When the music changes, so does the dance"
Hausa proverb

Until then, Christmas trips back to our village of Omuma in Nigeria to visit my maternal family had felt completely separate from my everyday reality. I hadn't quite connected personally with the gravity of the stories my parents told me about the 'Get The Darkies Out' petition launched on mum's street when she arrived in the UK having survived the horrific conflict of the Biafran war, or about the racism they faced as an interracial couple during their courtship. I had considered it a joke when my paternal grandma suggested the growing pains in my lower back were because my "spine wasn't sure whether to be African or European". As a child I had begged my mum to "wash the brown off me" in the bath and straighten out my afro curls to fit in with the other girls at school, but a few years later I had expressed to her that I wished I was "properly black, like you". For so long these were experiences I compartmentalised.

Let's get one thing straight: I am undoubtedly privileged, enjoying a safe and comfortable existence, and it is important to check that privilege regularly, using the responsibility it affords me to help others less fortunate where I can. I cannot pretend that I'll ever fully understand the struggles of the black experience in a world still so unjust and unequal. But 'White' is an exclusive club to which someone like me does not belong. Nor does it seem appropriate to identify, strictly-speaking, as 'Black', and growing up I felt like an outsider looking in on many aspects of black culture and community. The cornerstone of adolescence for every young person is a grapple with their sense of who they are; mine was underpinned by a yearning for wholeness.

But wholeness is not to be found in diluting one component of my racial heritage or the other; it is not, as my parents were advised, "deciding what colour to raise your kids", because they are not two dichotomous halves. We are not half-caste. For me, 'becoming' and 'belonging' has been about exploring my blackness and my whiteness as living, breathing, moving parts; confronting race as an issue head on, learning about it, talking about it, celebrating the beauty of my cultures, and being honest about the ugly parts of our history. Suggesting that we should be colourblind serves as a gross erasure, I believe, to our dynamic identities and lived experiences.

"Love does not begin and end the way we seem to think it does. Love is a battle, love is a war; love is a growing up."
James Baldwin, Nobody Knows My Name: More Notes of a Native Son

So to postulate where past relationships went wrong, I think it's likely that not talking about race or privilege played a key part. This attempt to conduct them in colour-blindness could be the root of their downfall. The shades were always there, but I'd watered down the palette. If we gravitate towards and form connections with others as an extension of our quest for a sense of self, then the grasp we have on our identity impacts the way we love. I guess for a long time I was looking for someone to love, and to love me to make me feel whole, and my partners' whiteness – in my eyes – symbolised a completeness and a sense of security I was lacking.

But the irony of this was that it led to so many other insecurities and a subtly corrosive power dynamic, which I've heard echoed by countless other friends in interracial relationships. I constantly felt inadequate and fetishised, studying my boyfriends' previous relationships (for the boys I dated between life in Newcastle and Cambridge, I was almost always the first non-white girl they'd been with) and feared that the novelty would soon wear off; that they'd leave me for someone more 'angelic': blonde, fair, petite. I self-loathingly stereotyped myself as a 'sassy', 'dramatic' mixed-race girl who'd surely become 'too much' for them. I'll never know if they felt any of that or not, but the anxiety is destructive.

"Lasting love has to be built on mutual regard and respect. It is about seeing the other person… Sometimes I can sense a blindness has set in. They have stopped seeing each other."
Chimamanda Ngozi Adichie

Celebrating my racial identity and consolidating my sense of self has been liberating, in so many ways. Notably, long gone is my 'type'. In fact, of late, there's been a fairly pronounced U-turn. Of course, there's a lot more choice in a sprawling, multicultural metropolis like London, and perhaps if I'd grown up here, dating Afro-Caribbeans, or men of any background, race or mix wouldn't feel like such a significantly different experience to what I've been used to. Conversations – particularly, about race – are enthralling: connecting with someone else who has felt like an outsider is invigorating, as there's solidarity in having experienced similar struggles and questioned ourselves in similar ways. A common understanding of the past, which bodes well for building a future together.

I find myself drawn to stories about love along colour lines, feverishly turning down pages in novels and making note of quotes (as littered throughout this essay) that articulate (in words that I previously couldn't find to describe a feeling that had once felt ephemeral) the ways in which race, prejudice, discrimination and cultural identity play a part in romance and relationships. We may have come a long way from the bigotry my parents faced as an interracial couple, we may be the future face of Britain, but as normalised as a mixed-race family may be my interest is nevertheless piqued when I see them in the street, or through a window. I'm ever curious as to the disparate stories and backgrounds that have come together, so often against all odds.

"The first generation does what the second doesn't want to.
The third is free to do what it likes"
Zadie Smith, NW

But what next? When it comes to starting a family and bringing children into the world, there was one particular concern deep inside me during my two long-term relationships that I never vocalised, for fear of echoing the sort of racism – or, goodness, eugenics – that motivated some people to oppose my parents' union in the first place. It is a concern insightfully investigated in the groundbreaking 2015 University of Kent paper entitled 'Keeping the story alive: Is ethnic and racial dilution inevitable for multiracial people and their children?', which focused on 64 parents, most of whom were first generation mixed-race with a white partner, discussing their children's identity.

Four key themes emerged: the loss in their children of "cultural knowledge" and their parents' ancestry; "the effect of physical markers of minority heritage not being present" or "white-appearing children"; a notion of "reduced racial fractions"; and "concerns about the loss of politicised racial consciousness". It's an interesting quandary. In the absence of significant new UK immigration, we will probably become largely absorbed into the wider white British community within a few generations. I wonder: what if my connection to my Nigerian heritage was not through my mother, but through a grandparent or great-grandparent? The shuffle of genes means that some will experience life - in a similar way as their mixed-race parent, and others will not how they're seen by others, their grapples with identity, their journey in love. Prompting the question: what will it mean to be mixed-race in the UK in 2030 or 2050? And, since we're talking coupling up, what will race have to do with who we fall for and who we end up with then?

> "Two people creating the time of their own lives,
> protected somehow by love, not ignorant of
> history but not deformed by it, either."
> Zadie Smith, Swing Time

Those who came before us fought for racial integration - including interracial marriage - because it is a good thing; it is the natural progression of a healthy society. I still believe that. But it can also result in a sense of loss. In fact, these two contradictory feelings will often exist side by side. One of the parents interviewed for the study succinctly expressed: "I don't want them to forget that race matters. That race affects people's life chances. I want them to help me and to help the world make it different".

So in response to whether love can - or should - ever be truly colourblind, I'd say no, on both counts. It is a beautiful thing that folk of different races are falling in love and building families and stories together, but it mustn't be because they 'don't see colour', because that would mean ignoring racism rather than combatting it. It would signify a dilution of our rich cultural heritage, which we have so many reasons to protect. This is not about what we look like to other people, it is what we know of ourselves. We need to be vocal and honest and proud, celebrating both the roots from which we have grown and the routes our lives are taking, especially as we move towards second and third-generation mixed-race. Because love can make us see life in a different colour, and colour can make us see love in a different light.

*Vick is a TV and Radio Presenter who has
previously hosted the Capital Breakfast Show on
Capital FM radio. She has also written for Marie
Claire and has published a children's novel 'Listen
Up: Rule the Airwaves, Rule the School'. Vick has
recieved a host of awards for her work and is an
ambassador for Amnesty International.*

Vick Hope

 @vicknhope

 @VickNHope

THE MYTH OF MARRIED BY 30

SHARMADEAN REID

I turned 30 all alone. I had recently moved back to my hometown of Wolverhampton, after having mild burnout following the rapid growth of my business, the breakdown of the relationship to my son's father and the mental overload of being a mother with a 3-year-old son in a big city without her family. Coming home saved me. After crashing in my little sister's spare room for a few months, I had finally found a home in my childhood neighbourhood. A large caretaker's house on a private road with a huge ancient garden, overlooking the canal. On my 30th birthday, the house had yet to be furnished. I woke up on May 28th in a bare room with a newly delivered bed and thin sheets. But I was content.

To combat the burnout I had tried a plethora of solutions both wacky and medical. I began biohacking by getting blood tests and stabilising my blood sugar to improve my mood. I began to learn about Myers Briggs personality types and the Enneagram. I tried yoga, a Columbian cacao drinking ceremony, I took herbal baths as recommended by Benedictine Monks, I had lots of facials, reiki, acupuncture and read books on 1970s vegetarianism. As was typical for someone who has crossed the first third of their life, I was searching for meaning, but for the first time in a long time, that meaning did not include a man.

The stillness and quietness and one-ness were visible in my healing. My body was strong and fit, my skin was glowing and I began to take a philosophical perspective to my life, as lived thus far. Being back home made it easier to spend time reading and learning, I was able to ask my family direct questions about my youth. Understanding that my childhood traumas had formed deep patterns in my relationships was like wiping off a dirty mirror. I could finally see myself and began to review the relationships I had had in my 20s and reflect on how much they had served me and my personal development. I began to spend my days connecting my self-reflection with philosophy, human biology, psychoanalysis and literature. It was thrilling. Naturally, I then longed for a partner to share this newfound wisdom with.

A year and a half later, and feeling somewhat ready to move back to London, I found a little flat in Ladbroke Grove. I cried as I left Wolverhampton for the last time and attempted to straighten my shoulders for the big city again. I realised that maintaining my All-One-Ness was going to be tough. Every Saturday morning I sat on the bar at Pizza East in Golborne Road surrounded by gorgeous European husbands and wives and children. The 'Married by 30 Myth' was starting to strike.

As my first delicious summer in West London rolled on, I was bombarded with stories on social media of the chic unions of cool young couples who had wed their post-university sweethearts. I began to get the Sunday Scaries... "I'm going to die alone", "No one wants me", "I'll never get married." The solution was pretty simple: eat breakfast somewhere else, get off the internet, and continue to read and work on myself.

The intervening years were filled with relationships that have acted as character devices in the film of my life. Dating post-30, as my friends start to pair off, has been interesting. There have been some casual relationships, some emotional ones, all united in the fact that I – ever loyal to my rapid pursuit of self-discovery – outgrew them all. These subplots were simply there to usher the story along as your heroine moves closer and closer to the self-love and actualisation that will make her able to love others. The most pertinent thing I learned during this period was to not act from my ego. To not act from the space when I am wounded, fearful, and closed. To not pretend that I am ready for marriage externally when I'm still trying to listen and love my core self.

I am still unmarried and happily so. I don't get those Sunday night voices and I continue to do the work. Each level of "work" peels back a layer while I am thrilled to expose. It gets me closer and closer to the kernel of myself.

The bar has been set high for my future husband. Not a bar of exhibitionist brunches and #relationshipgoals, but a bar whereby the initial rung admits that we are both flawed humans and accept each other as we come. Just above that bar, a union that enables us to use our relationship as a conduit to become better humans. And if you tilt your head way above that bar, a love that fulfils me as a woman, a lover, a mother, a wife.

Sharmadean Reid, MBE is the founder of Beautystack, a VC-backed platform that allows users to discover and book exciting beauty professionals. She is also the founder of Wah Nails and Future Girl Corp.

Sharmadean Reid

 @sharmadeanreid

 @sharmadeanreid

"WITHOUT DEVIATION FROM THE NORM, PROGRESS IS NOT POSSIBLE"

FRANK ZAPPA

TRADITIONS WORTH KEEPING AND OTHERS I'D LIKE TO CHANGE

EM CLARKSON

When I was first asked to be involved in this project, I was not engaged, nor was I expecting to be anytime soon. But rather conveniently, eight days after I agreed to write a chapter about my hypothetical wedding and the traditions I, as a modern feminist, would hypothetically be keeping, my boyfriend of seven years was down on one knee asking me to marry him and all of a sudden this chapter went from being a hypothetical imagining of "every little girl's fantasy" to being the very real question of what "this averagely sized feminist's reality" was going to look like.

Theoretical thoughts on "tradition" have become matters of practicality as much as anything else. And as it turns out, it's much easier to write off wedding traditions as a ridiculous example of the ways in which our capitalist society exploits these tragically misogynistic ideals when no one has asked you to marry them yet.

See, there's the **first tradition** that I feel I ought to have a problem with. The fact that as a woman I was just sort of meant to sit around and wait to be proposed to. That my father's permission needed to be sought out, as if I were a possession, or a commodity; something that could be traded for a luscious green field or a well fed pig. How my relationship would've been perceived had I taken it upon myself to ask the question I should've been asked.

That was suggested to me, on more than one occasion. Normally by older women barely disguising the pity they felt for me; a woman who'd been in a relationship for as long as I had, who still had nothing to show for it.

"You could always ask him, you know?", they'd say.

And I'd think about it; about stretching the parameters of equality in my own relationship and popping the question. But in the end I'd laugh it off, telling them that I wasn't in any rush, or even that bothered by marriage, and then I'd ask them if they wanted another drink and I'd scarper.

Harbouring these feelings alone, though, I think I'd have worried that I might be emasculating my man by proposing (the man that, when I met him had a stick of concealer and a tinted moisturiser), robbing him of the chance to fulfil his male prerogative and spend a small fortune on this piece of jewellery that, if I'm honest with myself, I just really wanted.

So yeah, if it got me a diamond I was willing to be a traditionalist. But what of the rest of it? When it comes down to it, what will my feminism mean for my nuptials?

Will I **wear a white dress** despite tradition dictating that it is an honour reserved for girls still pure, untouched, and who definitely haven't had a girls' holiday to Zanté?

Will **my father give me away** even though no one that knows either of us would be under any illusion that I might be his to give?

Will **I throw my bouquet** into a crowd of female friends, despite the fact that in doing so I am playing into the very idea that I resented for so long; that women are, deep down, all so desperate that they will physically fight one another for the chance at the security marriage will offer them?

I hadn't given an awful lot of thought to my wedding, before I got engaged. In fact, and I'm almost entirely sure this isn't something a person so recently betrothed is supposed to admit; if my boyfriend weren't religious and it weren't so important to him, it wouldn't have broken my heart to live a wedding-less life. I didn't race home to my childhood bedroom and haul out an overstuffed scrapbook that I'd been curating since I was a little girl so as to "finally" put the wheels in motion. In fact it was only after my best friend arrived at my house the day after I got engaged, armed with the promise of the best hen do ever(!) and ready to give me a crash course in Pinterest, that I started to give any serious thought to the things society assumes I've been dreaming of since well before my first period.

Namely flowers; I'm spending an almost alarming amount of time thinking about flowers. I'm also stumbling across traditions that I've decided I absolutely hate; how had I not noticed before that all the speeches at weddings were given by men? If I were the daughter of an oracle or marrying a poet this'd be a tradition I'd deny the crowds. The women in my life are quite simply too wonderful not to be heard.

The talk surrounding my "bridal party" (or my "Bride Tribe", as Pinterest keeps assuming I'd like to refer to it) I'm also taking issue with. Not necessarily on the grounds of misogyny or the somewhat legitimate issue of outdated gender stereotyping that surrounds women and weddings, but honestly because so much of it is just so naff.

Tradition also dictates, at least according to my mother, that my new husband and I might be expected to leave our wedding reception early to go and begin our new lives together, as man and wife. Now I may not know much about weddings, but I do know a lot about my relationship; and that's that it was solidified by our mutual loathing for leaving a party early. Tradition-Shmadition:

we will be there until the bitter end. Despite the fact that "no one likes a pissed up bride", apparently. That might just be another area in which we make some allowances.

There is a part of me that wonders why I'm even getting married, since I'm not religious or that resolute in my need to conform to the traditions. But then I think about my relationship and I find myself overflowing with love for a man that I can't wait to share my life with. I'd do anything for him. Drink a cocktail out of a penis shaped straw, take my life in my clumsy hands by wearing white all day and all night, be bartered for like a prize pig. I can't wait to celebrate our love. I can't wait for our wedding.

We'll make some changes; we are a modern couple in a modern relationship and neither of us wouldd expect me to promise before God, or anyone, to "obey" another person. But for the most part I find myself prepared to conform to the traditions that make weddings what they are.

Does that make me a bad feminist? I hope not.

I'll wear a veil because this might be my only chance to do so (unless my next marriage is into a drug cartel, where I hear the mourning period is rather fashionable) and I would be devastated to be robbed of that opportunity. I'll wear a floor length white dress for the same reason. My dad will walk me down the aisle because there's every chance I'd stack it if I journeyed alone. Also because, whether either of us would admit it, it'd break our hearts if he didn't. I might not be his property, but I am his eldest daughter and there's huge sentiment attached to that.

Perhaps I'm just another feminist falling victim to the patriarchal ideologies that claimed so many before me. Blinded by the sparkle from the ring on my left hand, signifying to the world that I have been claimed. Bagsied. Bought? Perhaps I'm exercising the rights my foremothers fought so hard for by cherry picking the parts of the tradition I want to carry through my new life? Perhaps I'm just in it for the party?

When I started this chapter I think I thought I'd be revolutionising the institution of marriage, breaking the mould and forging new traditions. As it turns out I'm just another peony-obsessed-Pinterest-whore ready to excitedly conform to these archaic traditions.

Em is a journalist, blogger and author who wants to create a space where women can 'be themselves totally unashamedly, whatever that may be.' As well as running the blog 'Pretty Normal Me', she is also the author of 'Can I Speak to Someone in Charge' and hosts a weekly podcast, also entitled 'Pretty Normal Me'.

Em Clarkson

 @em_clarkson

 @EmilyClarkson

I DON'T SEARCH, I FIND

LUKE DAY

I thought 2019 was a tough year. To call it challenging would be an understatement. I had my heart broken (more than once), I was getting divorced and to top it all off my house got broken into on my birthday. "Happy fucking birthday Luke, Love, The Universe." I felt like my personal space had been violated, and my home was stripped of some treasured valuables and jewellery. To any outsider, they were just replaceable material possessions, but for me, many of them held poignant, emotional memories.

Luke is the Fashion Director of GQ, the Editor of British GQ Style and freelance stylist. He describes himself as 'unapologetic, owning my sexuality, having fun dressing up and living my best life'.

Luke Day

@ @luke_jefferson_day

🐦 @LJDay

But 2019 turned out to be liberating, too. Although I was heartbroken by the events of last year, I found some comfort in the thought that sentiments live inside us, not the actual object. It was a symbolic moment to release my past life and see this as a cleansing; the beginning of a new chapter.

So I strode into 2020 with high expectations. I was ready to find the love of my life and I was certain I was going to nail that challenge like a boss. It would be fair to say that I took to dating with gay abandon. But even that categorisation was called into question — when, at one party, I was asked whether I was 100% gay. My response was swift: 'To be 100% gay is 100% boring.' It was a tongue-in-cheek quip, delivered off-hand, but the moment did give me pause for thought.

After being in conventional, monogamous relationships with men for all of my adult life (even marrying in a very hetero-idealised, conforming way), being single in 2020 has meant a new dating landscape with attitudes towards gender, sex and sexuality that would have been unrecognisable to me just a decade ago. So I set about exploring this unknown terrain with open-minded abandon.

Not long ago, I was briefly romancing a polyamorous man who taught me about consensual, ethical and responsible nonmonogamy. I spent most of a wild night making out with a lesbian. It reminded me that, while I've always identified as a gay man, I've had a great time having sex with women in the past. Could I be pansexual? Identifying as bisexual, meaning that you are attracted to two genders, had never appealed to me. Pansexuality feels a lot more interesting, given that being pansexual is about romantic or emotional attraction regardless of sex or gender identity. The possibilities are endless. Now, that's a real turn-on.

Gender, sex and sexuality are all pretty complicated ideas and definitely not as black and white as some people might think. Courage knows no gender. Love knows no limit. Sexuality is not a choice, it's a spectrum, and that's what I love most about life. The most magnetic people are those who live their truth, honestly. Authenticity is being a whole person and there's nothing sexier than that.

I'd only just begun to enjoy this new romantic freedom when the Covid-19 pandemic hit 2020, acting as the biggest cock block — suddenly we were all behind closed doors. At first, I felt lost. They do say that when one door closes, another one opens, but initially I didn't know where to find it because I was too busy chipping away at the door that was already slammed closed in my face. But then, I realised that the door I'd walked past and rejected too many times was the right one, and that the door to love opens inwards. Yes, ladies and gentleman, I found my true love in lockdown. It's me.

'THE DEMAND FOR EQUAL RIGHTS IN EVERY VOCATION OF LIFE IS JUST AND FAIR, BUT, AFTER ALL, THE MOST VITAL RIGHT IS THE RIGHT TO LOVE AND BE LOVED'

EMMA GOLDMAN

LOVE IN THE LYRICS
'YOU REALLY GOT A HOLD ON ME' – SMOKEY ROBINSON

ORSON FRY

If love is someone having a hold on you, no one sang it better and more believably than Smokey Robinson in this 1962 Motown classic. Unbelievably, it was originally released as a B-side to the now largely forgotten track 'Happy Landing,' so it was left to DJ's across the country to flip the record over. But when they did, it soared up the charts, becoming an R&B No.1 smash hit.

Lyrics aren't meant to be read, they're meant to be sung, and in this number it's all about Smokey's delivery. It's the pure anguish of being possessed. He wails (almost) reluctantly, caught in the grips of a cool, overpowering desire. It's love as sickness, love as a drug, and the lover as patient or junkie. A question of 'need' and not 'want.'

Smokey wrote the song on a business trip to New York while acting as vice-president for Motown's Tamla record label. He was bored in his hotel room and was trying to write a song in the manner of Sam Cooke's 'Bring It On Home To Me,' and came up with something much more special—an obsessive love ballad with lyrics that claw through the various emotions of an unreasonable passion. All it needed were harmonies from Bobby Rogers and those distinctive guitar lines from Marv Tarplin and Eddie Willis to create that unmistakable groove. It caught the attention of the Beatles who covered it on their second album 'With The Beatles,' and recorded it as late as 1969 during their Let It Be sessions.

Smokey has long credited Berry Gordy, the man behind the Motown Record Label, with teaching him how to give his songs continuity. To make them about one thing and then get to the essence of that thing. After 1962 Smokey would write dozens of Motown hits for his own group the Miracles and for other artists like Marvin Gaye and the Temptations, helping turn Motown into the most successful African-American owned business in America.

When responding to a question of 'which poets do you dig' in a 1965 televised press conference, Bob Dylan, in an interview otherwise marked by his non sequiturs and put-ons, suddenly looked serious for a second, and said "Smokey Robinson."

ON AN UNEXPECTED KNEE

EDWARD DOWNPATRICK

Why I, a man, am totally down with being proposed to and why I think other men should be too.

Is marriage outdated and inherently sexist? Is discussing an area in which women have historically had less power than men insensitive? Do plenty of women already propose to their boyfriends? Penning this piece quickly becomes redundant if we answer yes to any of these. This short essay is, broadly speaking, pro women, pro love, and anti the male centricity of the last two thousand odd years.

According to the Office of National Statistics and other such government agencies around the world, men are roughly twice as likely to be killed by the coronavirus than women. Women will survive longer in icy water than men. Their life expectancies tend to be higher than their sexual counterparts. By the evidence first and foremost of Angela Merkel but also the female leaders of Taiwan, New Zealand, Iceland, Finland, Norway, and Denmark (nod to HM The Queen here too) who have, though time will of course tell, more commendably handled this crisis than their male counterparts, they very possibly make for better leaders and it's almost beyond doubt that they make better doctors (I'll park the male-dominated realm of surgery for the sake of this argument). So goes the old expression, grow a pair of balls. Why on earth would that be a sensible means of toughening-up? A mere flick to the balls can incapacitate, but the female equivalent... undoubtedly more robust. I'm talking about childbirth people, come on. Fine, most men would best most women in a physical confrontation, and look, I'm yet to have the living daylights kicked out of me by a woman, but then again, I haven't met and miffed someone like Xena the Warrior Princess.

Why reflect on the musings of famous philosophers throughout the ages? Well, in part, because their thinking was so important it earned them their own adjectives, e.g., Platonic (relationship/thinking) after Plato, but also because their thinking serves to hold up a mirror to prevailing attitudes and views of the times. An extensive examination of the abject cruelty and act of species-self-harm that is sexism over the last two-and-a-half thousand years would take tomes and my mind is not worthy to act as guide, there being a mere handful of people with the time to plough through as much is another matter altogether.

Googling 'male philosopher feminists' is a bit like Googling French military victories. Aristotle believed women weak and inferior, not even of the same nature. That theme largely continues for a couple of thousand years but might have been elsewise. Plato argued that men and women in fact had the same nature, an equal capacity in the most esteemed practice of all – medicine, and the same responsibility to guardianship, both of the State and of the home. He believed in metempsychosis (essentially reincarnation), that the human soul was sexless and could change genders from life to life. He also argued that some women should be trained to rule. Plato, Republic: "If women are expected to do the same work as men, we must teach them the same things." Progressive thinking, fair thinking if you will, has always existed and with utmost justification.

If you progress through the philosophy of Rousseau, in which you would be forgiven for thinking him something of anti-feminist, he eventually makes it plain that if given the opportunity to shape society as men had, women could very well change the world. According to the revolutionary thinker, whatever biological differences between men and women existed, the so-called weaker sex had shown repeatedly that they were capable of greatness. Fast forward to today, the opportunity granted, the world enduringly changed.

Shakespeare, through his formidable female characters, evidently envisioned a much greater estate for womankind. So many of his plotlines' salvation from calamity, lunacy, and selfish folly so often came thanks to the strength, wit, and wisdom of a heroine. Rosalind in As You Like It, Viola in Twelfth Night, Beatrice in Much Ado About Nothing. To give the French some credit, Beaumarchais, in his exposure of the foibles of men (and it wasn't just of hapless, tyrannical aristocrats), also raises his female characters to the level of heroine. Just think of The Marriage of Figaro and The Barber of Seville.

From the time of Plato to present day, the state of woman has only really changed in a recent and very short space of time. Property rights (not being the property of a man, at least in more tolerant societies, notwithstanding), the right to vote, the right to perform the same societal functions, equal pay, well ok we're not quite there yet, but still. Given a similar stab, the same tools - take that manfolk, you're not actually all that. But it's not all about women becoming more equal to men, but men becoming able to be, dare I say it, more like women, child-rearing and bread-winning being the obvious examples. Does it make a man less of a man? Depends who you ask I suppose. Depends on the man in question. The better question to ask is, does it make them less of a person? Absolutely not. If anything, it elevates man to dissolve himself of his preconceived, gender-stereotyped role, remove the self and become more of a team player. How can this not improve relationships, both between spouses and between parents and children?

As an evolution to the argument propounded by and in the less-populous times of Plato, David Attenborough believes one of the keys to saving our planet is the education and emancipation of women around the world. It is the greatest non-authoritarian measure in the battle against resource scarcity. The former one-child policy in China, the breaking of which could be penalised with forced sterilisation, sits at the other end of the spectrum. Free women from the shackles of arranged marriages and domestic incarceration and you have a more balanced and industrious workforce, fewer children born, and therewith fewer mouths to feed.

It can only be an utterly exquisite thing for a man to be asked given the aeons-old role upended to so do.

What is the point of saying all of this given the title you read at the start of the piece (assuming of course that you have made it this far)? Minds immeasurably superior to mine have for the last two-and-a-half thousand years made the case and as does this lesser one now, that the world is irrefutably a better one when women, rightly elevated to equal footing, take full part. Ipso thus pro quo, a Frankenstein's monster of a sequitur, why shouldn't men be proposed to and why should they not want to be?

This brings us, herringing to the red somewhat, to the unquantifiable dimension, that which along with artistry raises us to the plane of blessed being – love. In Christopher Nolan's Interstellar love provides humanity the gateway to its salvation. It is raised to the level of fifth dimension. From the most ecstatic elation to the deepest pits of despair, the greatest acts of kindness, heroism, and sacrifice to the most despicable acts of cruelty and violence, love is the species-defining force driving us on. It does not belong to any one person, group, sex, faith or otherwise and it ought to be the overwhelming reason behind couples' decisions to marry. So why therefore should the keys to marriage be possessed by men alone. It has never been their sole possession, but its pretext has for time-immemorial been used as a societal whacking stick the oppressive likes for which our post-Neanderthal state has had no match.

This is not to say that men should en masse jettison their genuflectional intentions. What on earth, at least in the near term, would social media feeds be bereft of the nigh quotidian nauseum of an engagement? They're not all like that of course. But if marriage is an equitable estate wherein both parties agree to, inter alia, through thick and thin have and hold, love and cherish, and bodily worship each other, why should it matter who does the proposing? The commitment is not entered into lightly, for either party. It's the biggest intake of air either person is ever likely to take (unless they do in fact get in the ring with Xena the Warrior Princess) and let us therewith muse on a most admirable trait, not the exclusive preserve of humankind it ought be noted - courage. It takes courage for a man to ask, it takes courage for a couple to commit to the long term, and it takes utmost bravery and belief for the non-traditional party to pop the question. It can only be an utterly exquisite thing for a man to be asked given the aeons-old role upended to so do. What an extraordinary and humbling experience, how unifying, and how brilliant, to know the woman you love loves you quite so much. It might take balls to ask that special someone to marry you, but men are not their sole possessors, and accordingly, let yet another playing field levelled be. The world might just be the richer for it.

Eddy is an Oxford-educated linguist who worked in the worlds of finance and luxury cosmetics before founding Highlands-inspired brand, FIDIR. He lives and travels in Scotland and enjoys contributing to a broad range of publications.

Edward Downpatrick

 @eddydownpatrick

EMILY
AND CJ

EMILY YATES

Our love story doesn't have a fairy-tale beginning; we met on Tinder! At the time, I was presenting documentaries for BBC Three, and the night we matched was the eve of the second one being released. I was naturally nervous about the reception of it, and chatting to CJ took that away. He messaged me the next day to say he'd rushed home from work to watch it which, of course, earned him immediate brownie points! He asked whether I was celebrating that night, and offered to take me out if I was free. As I'd only recently moved to Glasgow, he took me on a drive of the surrounding areas on a little road trip of his life; he showed me where he grew up, went to school, worked and even the places he goes when he needs to think. We talked and laughed, and it was lovely to be involved in something a little different to a first date coffee. And the rest, as they say, is history (although I try to downplay the fact I met a total stranger after 24 hours of messaging him whenever my mum is around...)

A few months later, my twin sister was getting married in Spain, so CJ met every member of my slightly dysfunctional family in one go, taking it completely in his stride. I remember not just fancying him, but feeling really proud of the effort he was making for me. I love this man endlessly but, even better, I really like him as a person, Our morals and values are the same and he's a genuinely lovely gentle giant. What you see is what you get, and it's so refreshing that he doesn't need to put on a persona to impress.

I have cerebral palsy, and have been a full-time wheelchair user from the age of 9. I was brought up to be pretty fearless, but remained terrified of dating and relationships throughout my teens and early twenties. CJ often has to be more than a boyfriend, especially when I'm not feeling my best, but he's never once complained or thrown it back in my face in the middle of an argument. So, last year, I decided to do something for him in return that would hopefully express my appreciation and show him just how much I adore him... and propose!

CJ has three big loves, aside from me: food, gaming and our two cats, Buzz and Woody. To incorporate the latter two, I spent six weeks designing and making a retro platform game, with all four of us as characters. Player CJ would have to navigate through the levels, cuddling the boys and making them purr along the way, with my character waiting at the end, and our dialogue leading to the proposal on the final screen.

On the day of the proposal, CJ had breakfast in bed – probably the biggest surprise of them all as he does all the cooking – before driving to our local amusement arcade to win some tickets and buy hilariously cheap prizes. We then had pizza at his favourite restaurant, before driving towards St Andrews singing along to a playlist I'd made of all our favourite songs. Arriving at our home for the next two nights, a lodge with hot tub, sauna and a terrace with incredible views, I was just so excited to pop the question. Knowing he still didn't expect a thing, I placed the laptop on the table and he excitedly started to play the game, not quite believing his very untechnical girlfriend had made it!

When his character met mine on the penultimate screen, the penny dropped. He sobbed and sobbed, so much so that I was starting to think I'd messed up, and in a flood of tears he shouted 'YES!'

It was the most beautiful moment. There's still such a taboo when it comes to women proposing to their partners, but I found the lack of expectation, and the fact that CJ didn't suspect anything right until the very last moment, really liberating. And to be able to give something back to the man who bends over backwards for me on a daily basis was truly magical. Oh, and I got to choose my own engagement ring – real bonus! We used haribo rings for some fun photos post-proposal, but I now have a gorgeous watermelon tourmaline and diamond ring.

We are in no rush for the wedding and are just enjoying this moment, but I'm thinking pixelated characters of all our wedding guests would make great favours!

Emily is an accessiblity consultant, travel writer and presenter who currently writes for Globe Hopper Guides.

Emily Yates

 @emryates

 @EmilyRYates

Elizabeth is an award-winning author, journalist and broadcaster. Her memoir 'How to Fail: Everything I've Ever Learned From Things Going Wrong' is a Sunday Times top 5 bestseller and is accompanied by her podcast, 'How to Fail'. She has published a number of other works and is also a columnist for You Magazine.

Elizabeth Day

📷 *@elizabday*

🐦 *@elizabday*

TEN THINGS YOU (BY WHICH I MEAN I) ONLY KNOW AS A DIVORCÉE

ELIZABETH DAY

1. You never think it will be you. When you're walking down the aisle on your wedding day, you might feel a tiny grain of discomfort, like a pebble in your shoe, but you will dismiss this and attribute it to nerves. You do not believe your marriage will end in divorce, of course you don't. But when it does, you won't be wholly surprised either.

2. When you are married, you will try very hard to make it work. So hard. You will try and try and try. You will explain and when that doesn't work, you will argue, and then you will cry because you hate to fight, and the whole process will repeat itself in endless cycles. You do not have anything to compare marriage with, so you think this is normal. It isn't.

3. It will take you a long time to confide in your best friend (to whom you normally tell everything) about what is going on behind closed doors. When you do, you are surprised how relieved you feel that she doesn't think less of you. That she has, in fact, been waiting for you to say something. You feel stronger because of her.

4. Telling your husband you are leaving him will be one of the scariest things you will ever do. But instinct will push you to do it, anyway. It will push you far beyond any comfort zones you ever imagined you had. At some point, you know that you have to leave or you will end up losing yourself; you will erase all your wants and needs and desires in order to stay silent and pliant and nice and not kick up a fuss. You know, deep inside, that this is not the way you want to live.

5. When you walk out of your marital home for the last time, you will feel strangely calm. This feeling will last for several weeks, until you realise it is actually numbness and that you are in shock. You will be able to operate completely normally on the surface, but you are not sleeping much and you are slightly late for everything and your best friend says it's like speaking to you through a perspex screen.

6. You will feel shame, even if it's misplaced. Other people will make you feel shame, until you realise it is not their life you're living. It is yours.

7. When the shock subsides, you are astounded by the beautiful gifted freedom of a second chance. You realise that it is never too late to change your life, and you are amazed by this, by the fact that you hadn't learned this lesson earlier.

8. It will take you a year to believe you made the right decision, but that doesn't mean you haven't. He will try and persuade you that you are making a terrible mistake. His friends will write you unkind emails. You come to terms with the fact that some people do not like you because they think they know the truth, but they never will. You gain strength from the knowledge that your truth lies beyond their perception of it. You stop explaining yourself, because you don't have to. You can just be.

9. It will take you a long time to remove your wedding ring. That's ok. You will have flings with men that seem more important than they are. That's ok too. Love that is ready is waiting for you to be ready for it.

10. The people you were most worried about letting down? They will be the ones who love you the most.

LOVE IN THE LYRICS
'BECAUSE THE NIGHT' –
PATTI SMITH

ORSON FRY

At some point in her life, Patti Smith needed a hit. Hard to imagine now that she's fully established herself as a punk rock heroine, and regularly travels the world playing sold out shows to adoring fans. But it was 1977 and Patti Smith needed a hit.

'Because The Night' belonged to Bruce Springsteen, who wrote the music and the chorus but was struggling with the verses. After four months of mumbling nothing much other than the song title itself in his recording sessions for Darkness on The Edge of Town, he gave up on it as an album track. A keen-eared and then still green sound engineer working with Springsteen, Jimmy Iovine (this was long before he would become one of the most important record executives in modern music) recognized the song's potential and asked Springsteen if he could give it to Smith whose album he was producing. "If she can do it, she can have it"[2] was his response. And she could do it, but she had to hear it first.

The song existed suspended in New York between two legends, waiting to be finished. Patti was more interested in her long-distance relationship with Fred Sonic Smith (guitarist from the MC5) than she was focused on a cassette now collecting dust in her apartment. Living two Great Lakes and 600-odd miles away meant Patti would wait by the phone for Fred to call. A lack of money and expensive phone calls resulted in the lovebirds talking "like once a week" - and so it was that she would sit by the phone willing it to ring. Often though it was Jimmy on the end of the line, asking whether she'd listened to the song yet? "I will I will I will" she'd respond but she wouldn't or didn't until one night Fred wasn't calling at the agreed 7:30pm time, and she was pacing around the room beside herself.

"There are certain things in my past I can't remember but this I remember second by second. I stood there, and I shook my head, and I might have even said out loud it's one of those darn songs."

"Fred didn't call me until almost midnight, but by midnight I had written all the lyrics." And so we were gifted one of the greatest expressions of longing and lust, because the night truly does belong to lovers.

---

[2] All quotes taken from the article - Patti Smith on 'Because The Night' at 40: How Her Bruce Springsteen Collaboration Is 'A Whole Life in A Song'

DIGITAL DATING IN THE AGE OF DISASTER

OLIVIA PETTER

It has never been easier to find someone to date. Pick up a smartphone, swipe your fingers, think of something funny to say and within an hour or so you could be on your way to sinking into a bottle of merlot with Luke, 28, from Hinge. At least, that's the myth we've been sold. In actual fact, today's dating landscape is such a labyrinth of angst, deceit and disappointment that it's tempting to give up altogether. Take dating app profiles. The very concept relies on duplicity: you have your real self – the one that cannot be squashed into filtered photos and inane jokes – and the self you can create to be as attractive as possible. This sets the precedent for the veil of inauthenticity that envelops the modern dating scene: match with someone, exchange jokes you've spent hours thinking about, meet in a pub one week later, have average-to-poor sex. Repeat.

But this boilerplate for modern love was shattered in March 2020, when the UK was hit by a pandemic. Suddenly, everything we thought we knew about dating changed. What was once a culture dominated by the superficial became peppered with verisimilitude. Physical pulls and burning urges were replaced with emotional bonds and intellectual connections, probably formed on Zoom or House Party. In this new dating landscape, it didn't really matter how tall you were, how big your muscles were, or whether you worked as a waiter or a chef.

Because chances were, you'd dyed your hair out of boredom and had recently been furloughed. All that mattered was connecting with someone. Having someone to make you laugh when you ran out of toilet roll. Finding someone to talk to late into the night when you couldn't sleep because the neighbours were having another fight. When the world was in lockdown, the physical element of a relationship was removed, meaning people had no choice but to focus on other things. Like how someone sounded when they spoke about their family, or how their body language changed depending on how comfortable they felt, and so forth. These are details we might've once missed in the drunken haze of a great first date, when all you can think about is how long until you get to tumble into each other's arms.

The pandemic ruptured the rituals for romance in more ways than one. It brought us back to a different era entirely. With physical relationships off the table, casual sex was replaced with courting, with people spending far longer getting to know one another than they otherwise would. And things that might have been dealbreakers suddenly didn't matter anymore – nothing like a global crisis to put things into perspective. Interestingly, despite all of these new barriers to love, people were getting deeper with one another than ever before. While doing research for my job at The Independent, where I host a podcast called Millennial Love, I heard from single people who had had dinner dates on Zoom, conducted virtual cocktail making classes on House Party, and even watched films together while miles apart (did you know Netflix has a feature that lets you do this?). These people found themselves opening up to total strangers about family feuds, past traumas and their deepest insecurities. Things they never would have spoken about so early on. Astonishingly, some couples were even sensing the moment when, were they on a real date, they would kiss. Had the dating scene finally been given the authenticity wake-up call it so desperately needed? And if so, why did it take a pandemic to trigger it?

Here's the thing. Vulnerability breeds intimacy: the minute you open up to someone, it creates a bond. The pandemic threw everyone off-kilter. It was bigger than all of us. We could not control it, nor could steer the government into giving us clarity on how long it would take to create a vaccine, or when the lockdown would be lifted. Even the most resilient among us were shaken up. But we were in it together, and desperate to talk to someone about our fears and anxieties. So we did, and despite the fact we weren't able to be with anyone outside our house, it brought people closer together than ever before... especially single people.

But not everyone's experiences of virtual dating went quite so smoothly. One man I spoke to found the whole thing painstakingly awkward. The conversation felt stilted, he said, and it was strange seeing someone's bedroom when you haven't met them yet, likewise them seeing yours. I also spoke to a young woman, let's call her Kate, who explained how she had been going on virtual dates with a man, let's call him Joseph, whom she had met shortly before the lockdown was imposed. They'd kept things up with regular phone calls and

FaceTime meetings until he proposed a "proper" date, or at least, as proper as one could be between two people behind screens. There would be cocktails, Kettle Chips and Penne Pomodoro, but from the comfort of their respective homes. When the time finally rolled around for the date, Kate phoned Joseph. He didn't answer. She tried again. Nothing. Two more unanswered calls and a series of unread WhatsApp messages later, it became clear that Joseph was no longer interested in dating Kate at all. He had blocked her.

You'd think that given we are living through one of the most deadly pandemics in modern history, people would be a little kinder to one another. But this is not always the case. We know that cruel behaviour such as ghosting, benching and breadcrumbing is rife on the modern dating scene, and that it has been exacerbated by digital technologies – you couldn't orbit someone (when the person who ghosted you continues to watch your Instagram stories) if you didn't have Instagram, for example. Plus, people who meet on apps often see their matches as disposable, which is understandable when you consider that your next date is only a swipe away. But when you amplify this by dating someone virtually like we had to in lockdown, it can foster an even greater culture of cruelty. Because when you are talking to someone you know you won't meet in-person, your behaviour feels more inconsequential, and so people are more callous.

The pandemic has exposed a different side to humanity, one that cannot conceal its fragility with an Instagram filter. And it has done the same for digital dating. While people are still able to connect, and some have, lockdown has inflamed the many negative behaviours that define how we date today.

All this raises further questions about the future of digital dating in a post-coronavirus world. Will people be kinder to those they meet on apps? Will single people prioritise finding emotional and intellectual connections over physical ones? And will falling in love with someone you met online ever carry the same serendipitous euphoria of falling in love with someone you met in the real world?

Olivia is a journalist at the Independent where she specialises in writing about the future of dating and relationships. She is the host of the chart-topping #MillennialLove podcast.

Olivia Petter

 @oliviapetter8

@Oliviapetter1

THE TIME I FELL IN LOVE WITH FIFTEEN WOMEN

POLLY VERNON

In the summer of 2015, I fell dramatically out of love with modern feminism. I'd published a book which celebrated women - in all our funny, brilliant, contradictory, beautifully flawed, endlessly complicated, often dickish, ultimately charming humanity – and politely asked if it was possible to be a feminist while aspiring toward sexiness, while basking in, and even actively inviting, male attention (because, spoiler alert, that's how I rolled). I'd called it Hot Feminist. Social media did not appreciate my contribution to the greater discussion surrounding gender politics. It was, at the time, particularly attached to the idea that feminism was a pure and serious business, that girls and women were only ever the victims of male attention, that being called 'love' by your male dry cleaner was an act of micro aggression perpetuated by the dark powers of the patriarchy, and that women's magazines (like the ones for which I regularly wrote) were hell bent on diminishing their readers' sense of self-worth, one pseudo cellulite cure at a time. My suggestion that there might be room for another strain of feminism, less interested in bemoaning millennia of suppression, more interested in wearing great clothes and focussing our efforts on specific ends - say, the shoring up of abortion rights – did not tickle social media's fancy. Not one bit.

I was subject to a process with which we've since become very familiar: a Twitter shaming. I was ridiculed and vilified online, discredited and undermined by thousands of people (only it felt like hundreds of thousands of people), the majority of whom were women who considered themselves feminists, and hadn't read my book.

Because I'd written Hot Feminist with what I have subsequently come to recognise as an unwise degree of honesty, because I'd gone into detail about who I was, and where I'd come from, the small battles I'd fought, how I'd been formed - this hurt. More than hurt. It depressed me. As in: I became actually, properly depressed for the months that followed publication; leaden, sad, anxious, intensely self critical, really rather lost. While some reviews were kind, and some readers enthusiastic, I was uniquely attuned to the negative. I emerged from this bleak time thoroughly disenchanted by modern feminism. If this was it – this cruel, dismissive, excluding and exclusive rabble which took such pleasure in decrying a woman on the basis she'd admitted she didn't necessarily mind getting her bum checked out on the street – then I was Out.

I recovered, but remained - quietly, residually - angry and hurt. Whenever anyone spoke, joyfully, of 'the sisterhood', I felt another twinge of anxiety and pain. If there truly was a sisterhood: why didn't it want me? What was wrong with me? Was the sisterhood only open to those who said exactly the right things, in exactly the right way? And if so, wasn't that demanding a level of mindless, unquestioning compliance feminism itself should revile?

That anger, and confusion, and sense of injustice stayed with me, and built and built, and I didn't really know what to do with it... And then, in the summer of 2016, the British boxer Nicola Adams won gold at the Rio Olympics. This shouldn't have meant anything to me. I didn't care for sports generally, and had less than zero interest in boxing - had never even thought about it TBH. Why should I give a damn about the triumph of this woman, even if she did seem to be a bewitching, coiled spring of energy, in her shorts and her gloves, with a smile that made the sun come out, and an extraordinary, world-beating talent?

By the winter of 2016, the part of my psychology that Adams had tweaked, had grown more compelling, more insistent. I found myself increasingly consumed by what I could only describe as "the desire to hit things". I now think some part of my brain had taken the wrath and pain Twitter had caused me, conflated it with the image of Nicola Adams' triumph, and concocted a plan.

The urge got stronger, and stronger. I expressed it to my friend and neighbour Helen.

"I really want to hit stuff, Hels," I said.

"I know exactly what to do with you," she replied.

And so it was that, on the first Saturday morning of January 2017, I found myself in the extraordinary environment of Islington Boxing Club, North London. My local community boxing gym: two rickety stories of corrugated iron walls, a leaking roof and a floor engorged with the literal blood, sweat and tears of decades and decades of true fighters. Its clientele includes champion fighters and Hollywood superstars, its whiff is so potent and distinct I'd know it anywhere, and its vibe is so masculine I couldn't quite believe I was allowed in.

But I was allowed in. More than that: I was welcomed. That's precisely what it, and so many community gyms like it, do. They welcome in anyone who needs them.

Helen had been coming to Islington Boxing Club to train on and off for years, since she was a teenager, and had more recently started attending the club's weekly women's only recreational sessions - to which she'd brought me. The group was lead by a trainer and a boxer called Sunni: an intensely charismatic foul-mouthed Australian ex model in possession of a body which immediately made me want to do whatever the hell it was she was doing, in the interest of acquiring something similar, on whom, I developed an instant, violent girl crush. This was useful: my consuming desire to impress Sunni meant I ignored the fact every molecule in my body was telling me to run away from this terrifying-seeming, deeply alien environment - not to mention, what would turn out to be a workout so intense, I kept thinking I was going to be sick.

Following half an hour's warm up and circuit training and star jumping and backward lunging and what felt like general impossible hell to me – a woman who hadn't attempted cardio since school – we got to the hitting stuff bit.

Now, I am not what you would call "a natural boxing talent". I am uncoordinated and was, at that point in time, pretty unfit; a skinny, weedy little thing who didn't do elevated heart rates by choice. But the first moment I raised my fist (nestled at that moment in an ugly blue borrowed boxing glove), twisted my hip as Sunni directed, swung my arm at one of the club's dangling punch bags, and landed my first jab, my world changed. Something in my nervous system, my muscles, my heart and my soul, wanted me to do this. Again and again and again! It was as if part of me had been missing, and I'd had no idea, but I'd just found it, in a smelly, ramshackle, beautiful boxing club, seven minutes round the corner from my house. I felt elated. And fulfilled. And less angry than I had in the time since social media had come to get me and my book.

So I went back the next week. And I went back, the week after that. And so on. I got fitter and stronger than I knew I could be. I got quicker, and I got tougher. I got a whole new understanding of what it means to be able to stand up for yourself. Social media's scorn bothered me less and less. Any time anyone kicked off online, I found myself thinking: "If you and I ever met, I could hit you, and it would hurt", and that, alone, made me care far less than I would have done in the past.

If boxing was a revelation, so were the women with whom I boxed.

It took us a while to bond; months to progress to the stage where we – the regulars, the 15 or so of us who turned up on those Saturday mornings, more often than not – would go for a coffee after class. It took a little longer for us to start exchanging gags on the WhatsApp group we shared. A year, till our first big night out. But slowly, slowly, we got there: to a point where we trusted each other enough to share the shit of the preceding week. Or the joy. Or the laughs. Or the hope. Someone began a relationship, we advised on the wording and composition of crucial early text messages. Someone else ended a relationship, we silently, sweatily hugged her when she cried in-between burpee reps. Someone who'd given up on the idea of sex altogether following a divorce got put on Tinder by three of the others - and discovered that sex had definitely not given up on her. Someone else got pregnant, we rejoiced: "We're having a baby! Our first baby!"

We got drunk together. We went on holiday together. We Zoom-trained together through the lockdown of 2020.

If I were to grow self-regarding, indulgent, and pseudo-anthropological about us, I'd perhaps say we're a fine example of modern Britain at its most progressive and functional. We are the most stupendously diverse group of women you could imagine. We're diverse in ways I did not know people could be diverse: age, fitness level, ethnicity, professions, class, body type, politics, sexuality, nationality and sensibilities. Our perspectives and experiences and world views are totally different. We're a walking, skipping, punching, coffee-drinking cultural cross section of womanhood in the UK - a focus-group coordinator's wet dream.

And we argue! Of course we argue. We have disagreed about everything, from trans activism to Brexit to (ha) feminism to how long you should wait before sleeping with someone... Everything, that is, apart from how much we love boxing, and how much we adore each other.

And if I were to grow analytical about us, I'd probably try to work out what it is that makes us so solid as a group. I might speculate it's because the endorphins we release while training leave us in such good spirits, we'd get on with anyone: an hour of boxing with Sunni, and we might as well have all come up on MDMA. I might wonder if there is something about women who are driven to learn to box, despite the fact it is still very much a male-dominated sport and space, despite the fact it's not considered a feminine pursuit, despite the fact it builds your body to a point where it looks useful, capable, dangerous and strong as opposed to traditionally sweetly pretty. that we recognise and respect in one another. I might think it's just 'cos we're all very funny.

Or maybe, I'd decide, it's that we're the mythical sisterhood - the one in which I'd lost all faith - in a different form. A physically and emotionally empowering, endlessly supporting, unquestioningly devoted, inherently female entity, which might not kill for each other, precisely... Except, then again, it might.

I wouldn't cross us on a dark night.

Ultimately, who cares? We are us. We get on. More than get on: we belong to each other. We just do. A big fat bunch of hard-training, sweat-dripping, coffee-crazed, lycra-clad women, who make each other laugh.

Polly has been one of the leading voices in debates on feminism and fashion for the past 15 years. She is a the Editor-At-Large and a columnist at Grazia and author of 'Hot Feminist'. Throughout her career Polly has written extensively for titles including The Guardian, The Observer, Vogue and The Evening Standard.

Polly Vernon

 @pollyvernon

 @PollyVernon

'LOVE IS OF ALL
PASSIONS THE
STRONGEST,
FOR IT ATTACKS
SIMULTANEOUSLY
THE HEAD,
THE HEART AND
THE SENSES'

LAO TZU

LOVE IN THE LYRICS
'INTO MY ARMS' – NICK CAVE

ORSON FRY

I remember first hearing Nick Cave's 'Into My Arms' and being swept up by the beauty of the tune and its lyrics. There's a hymn-like quality to the song which perhaps shouldn't surprise us. Introducing it at a concert in 1999, Cave said he'd written it outside a little country church in Surrey: "I was skulking up the back listening to the vicar banging on about this and that, and I went outside and wrote this."

When Cave was growing up in the northeast region of Victoria, Australia, he served as a choir boy in the local Anglican cathedral. He's since maintained close ties to faith and often mines the Bible for material in his songwriting. In 'Into My Arms' he plays with the interesting narrative technique of 'I don't believe, but if I did,' and goes on to explain what he'd do if he did believe in an Interventionist God and the existence of angels. Without giving too much away, it amounts to a rich and original statement of his love—but not an altogether happy one.

At 19, Cave lost his father in a car accident, an event he's since maintained as the catalyst for propelling him on the artistic path. Sorrow swamps his songs, even the ones about love. This might explain why some people hear 'Into My Arms' as a love song, and others as a song about loss. But, as Cave would tell us, the two things are inseparable: "The love song is not simply happy" he once wrote, "It must first embrace the potential for pain... within its melody, its lyric, it must sense an acknowledgement of its capacity for suffering."[1] With its plunging, haunting melody and its chant-like nature, Cave pulls this off so masterfully in 'Into My Arms.' And as we hear in that last rapturous verse, it is the God of Love who finally gets the upper hand.

---

[1] From 'The Secret Life of Love Songs' – two lectures prepared by Cave for the 1998 Vienna Poetry Festival

POETRY

SONNET 116

WILLIAM SHAKESPEARE, 1609

Let me not to the marriage of true minds
Admit impediments. Love is not love
Which alters when it alteration finds,
Or bends with the remover to remove.
O no! it is an ever-fixed mark
That looks on tempests and is never shaken;
It is the star to every wand'ring bark,
Whose worth's unknown, although his height be taken.
Love's not Time's fool, though rosy lips and cheeks
Within his bending sickle's compass come;
Love alters not with his brief hours and weeks,
But bears it out even to the edge of doom.
If this be error and upon me prov'd,
I never writ, nor no man ever lov'd.

MY HEART'S FIT TO BREAK

LADY CAROLINE LAMB, 1785-1828

My heart's fit to break, yet no tear fills my eye,
As I gaze on the moon, and the clouds that flit by;
The moon shines so fair, it reminds me of thee,
But the clouds that obscure it are emblems of me.

They will pass like the dreams of our pleasures and youth,
They will pass like the promise of honor and truth,
And bright thou shalt shine when these shadows are gone,
All radiant, serene, unobscur'd-but alone.

WHEN WE TWO PARTED

LORD BYRON, 1788-1824

When we two parted
In silence and tears,
Half broken-hearted
To sever for years,
Pale grew thy cheek and cold,
Colder thy kiss;
Truly that hour foretold
Sorrow to this.

The dew of the morning
Sunk chill on my brow-
It felt like the warning
Of what I feel now.
Thy vows are all broken,
And light is thy fame:
I hear thy name spoken,
And share in its shame.

They name thee before me,
A knell to mine ear;
A shudder comes o'er me-
Why were thou so dear?
They know not I knew thee,
Who knew thee too well:-
Long, long shall I rue thee,
Too deeply to tell.

In secret we met-
In silence I grieve,
That thy heart could forget,
Thy spirit deceive.
If I should meet thee
After long years,
How should I greet thee?-
With silence and tears.

A BRIDAL SONG

PERCY BYSSHE SHELLEY, 1821

The golden gates of Sleep unbar
Where Strength and Beauty, met together,
Kindle their image like a star
In a sea of glassy weather!
Night, with all thy stars look down, -
Darkness, weep thy holiest dew, -
Never smiled the inconstant moon
On a pair so true.
Let eyes not see their own delight; -
Haste, swift Hour, and thy flight
Oft renew.

Fairies, sprites, and angels, keep her!
Holy stars, permit no wrong!
And return to wake the sleeper,
Dawn, - ere it be long!
O joy! O fear! what will be done
In the absence of the sun!
Come along!

LOVE AND FRIENDSHIP

EMILY BRONTE, 1818-1848

Love is like the wild rose-briar,
Friendship like the holly-tree,
The holly is dark when the rose-briar blooms
But which will bloom most contantly?
The wild-rose briar is sweet in the spring,
Its summer blossoms scent the air;
Yet wait till winter comes again
And who will call the wild-briar fair?
Then scorn the silly rose-wreath now
And deck thee with the holly's sheen,
That when December blights thy brow
He may still leave thy garland green.

THE DEATH OF LOVERS

CHARLES BAUDELAIRE

There shall be couches whence faint odours rise,
Divans like sepulchres, deep and profound;
Strange flowers that bloomed beneath diviner skies
The death-bed of our love shall breathe around.

And guarding their last embers till the end,
Our hearts shall be the torches of the shrine,
And their two leaping flames shall fade and blend
In the twin mirrors of your soul and mine.

And through the eve of rose and mystic blue
A beam of love shall pass from me to you,
Like a long sigh charged with a last farewell;

And later still an angel, flinging wide
The gates, shall bring to life with joyful spell
The tarnished mirrors and the flames that died.

TO SOME LADIES

JOHN KEATES, 1884

What though while the wonders of nature exploring,
I cannot your light, mazy footsteps attend;
Nor listen to accents, that almost adoring,
Bless Cynthia's face, the enthusiast's friend:

Yet over the steep, whence the mountain stream rushes,
With you, kindest friends, in idea I rove;
Mark the clear tumbling crystal, its passionate gushes,
Its spray that the wild flower kindly bedews.

Why linger you so, the wild labyrinth strolling?
Why breathless, unable your bliss to declare?
Ah! you list to the nightingale's tender condoling,
Responsive to sylphs, in the moon beamy air.

'Tis morn, and the flowers with dew are yet drooping,
I see you are treading the verge of the sea:
And now! ah, I see it, you just now are stooping
To pick up the keep-sake intended for me.

If a cherub, on pinions of silver descending,
Had brought me a gem from the fret-work of heaven;
And smiles, with his star-cheering voice sweetly blending,
The blessings of Tighe had melodiously given;

It had not created a warmer emotion
Than the present, fair nymphs, I was blest with from you
Than the shell, from the bright golden sands of the ocean
Which the emerald waves at your feet gladly threw.

For, indeed, 'tis a sweet and peculiar pleasure,
(And blissful is he who such happiness finds,)
To possess but a span of the hour of leisure,
In elegant, pure, and aerial minds.

WE ARE MADE ONE WITH WHAT WE TOUCH AND SEE

OSCAR WILDE, 1854-1900

We are resolved into the supreme air,
We are made one with what we touch and see,
With our heart's blood each crimson sun is fair,
With our young lives each spring-impassioned tree
Flames into green, the wildest beasts that range
The moor our kinsmen are, all life is one, and all is change.
And we two lovers shall not sit afar,
Critics of nature, but the joyous sea
Shall be our raiment, and the bearded star
Shoot arrows at our pleasure! We shall be
Part of the mighty universal whole,
And through all Aeons mix and mingle with the Kosmic Soul!
We shall be notes in that great Symphony
Whose cadence circles through the rhythmic spheres,
And all the live World's throbbing heart shall be
One with our heart, the stealthy creeping years
Have lost their terrors now, we shall not die,
The Universe itself shall be our Immortality!

WILD NIGHTS! WILD NIGHTS!

EMILY DICKINSON, 1891

Wild nights! Wild nights!
Were I with thee,
Wild nights should be
Our luxury!

Futile the winds
To a heart in port, –
Done with the compass,
Done with the chart.

Rowing in Eden!
Ah! the sea!
Might I but moor
To-night in thee!

WHEN YOU ARE OLD

WILLIAM B. YEATS, 1893

When you are old and grey and full of sleep,
And nodding by the fire, take down this book,
And slowly read, and dream of the soft look
Your eyes had once, and of their shadows deep;
How many loved your moments of glad grace,
And loved your beauty with love false or true,
But one man loved the pilgrim Soul in you,
And loved the sorrows of your changing face;
And bending down beside the glowing bars,
Murmur, a little sadly, how Love fled
And paced upon the mountains overhead
And hid his face amid a crowd of stars.

'To be loved is a
privilege, to love
is a human right'

Pandora Sykes, 'In Conversation'

FUTURE

A BLACK
LOVE STORY

BINWE ADEBAYO

When I was little, Sunday mornings were always the same. My dad would go out to get the newspaper, and once settled in his favourite spot, would spend the day there, accompanied only by a cup of tea and a football game on in the background. My mom would sift through her impressive collection of cassette tapes and CDs and inevitably land on Donny Hathaway, Whitney Houston or Luther Vandross. Powerful, passionate RnB vocals would pulse through our house, and by the time I was 10 I knew all the words to songs about love found, lost or thrown away. Black love has always had an expressive soundtrack. In a complicated history, characterised by silence, survival and the search for sanctuary; black love has propelled itself through the ages through various expressive forms.

And that's what makes the 'concept' of black love difficult to write about; that it's not an inherent, inalienable category, recognisable everywhere from Amsterdam to Abidjan. Instead, like many parts of oppressed black life, it has found its home in forms of art and resistance. Genres like the blues, gospel, RnB and hip hop have allowed black love to have a voice, words and a place in our imagination. The famous singer and activist Nina Simone said that she did not play jazz, she played "black classical music"; an ode to the quality, precision and uniqueness of black musical expression. And these expressive genres were critical to the survival of black love.

Historically, mainstream media, as well as television and film, has actively left black love out of the story. As the critical race theorist Melissa Harris-Perry examines, black life (particularly when we're talking about women) has been presented in narrow, constricting stereotypes, and very little examination of our private lives. Much like Shylock in The Merchant of Venice, appealing to the humanity of Jewish people, generic depictions of black people often leave out their hurt, their interpersonal relationships and their love stories. While the 'poor but happy family' trope has been trotted out regularly to make white audiences feel better about themselves, black relationships (particularly romantic ones) have been primarily depicted through black-created forms of work.

In our literary history, writers like James Baldwin, Toni Morrison, Teju Cole and Chimamanda Ngozi Adichie have inscribed black family life into their books and in doing so, tackled the ways in which black love has had to protect itself from a world hostile to its development. This means dealing with the ways that racism and racist segregation has spatially affected black lives. For immigrant and African diaspora writers, it has meant engaging with mixed-heritage parents and third culture children, whose blackness is the product of various cultural outlooks. And for all of these stories, our particular culturally-specific gestures of love have been allowed to descend through generations, giving black love a meaningful personal footprint, even as it continues to be erased, marginalised or distorted for those who reject the full humanity of black people.

Musicians like Billie Holiday, Miriam Makeba and Bob Marley intermingled their very public politics of civil rights with delicate storytelling of their own private love woes. After all, in both the contexts of America's Jim Crow Laws and South Africa's brutal apartheid state, love was political. Indeed, loving the wrong person with the wrong hue could get you killed. This tension, bottled up within generations of black artists, has spilled into our creativity over and over, and our love story continues to live somewhere in between a happy melody and a funeral fugue.

And more so as industries become (marginally) more diverse, film and television have been shaped by, and in turn shape, depictions of what black love and romance really look like. Black Directors like Spike Lee and more recently Barry Jenkins, Ava DuVernay and Jordan Peele have fought against a sea of cookie-cutter 'highschool sweetheart' narratives to inject stories about the ways in which black people court one another, negotiate familial dynamics and commune with one another. And even amongst the black community, that still has to surmount massive challenges around homophobia, transphobia, ableism and the like; films like Moonlight – which depicts the life and struggles of a gay, black boy living in 'the hood', and the reality that blackness itself also excludes, judges and constricts – demonstrates that the battle for love to really win is inevitably fought from within and without.

And sure, these cultural artefacts are a fragmented effort at telling the story of black love; together they make a huge impact on their audiences. For many black people in their 20s, who would've grown up in the 90s and early 2000s, depictions of black love, romance and sex gained mainstream space through RnB and hip-hop music videos. 20 minute long multi-part (almost telenovela style) videos would show the pursuit, the connection and the eventual disruption. The idea of the JLo-Ja Rule 'keeping it real' couple, or Beyoncé-Jay Z glam 'it couple' were delightful peeks into what our romantic futures (with black partners) could be if we found 'the one'. Elsewhere, the emergence of 'gangsta rap' and the video vixen era spearheaded by artists like 50 Cent also showed us that black love could represent a tricky transactional relationship where black women's sexuality was their purpose in these contexts, and the way in which they gained favour with their male counterparts. Elsewhere still, shows like The Cosby's and The Fresh Prince of Bel-Air showed that black love could be synonymous with a stable, nuclear family and the ability to express love through high-value material gifts.

Now, I'm not making a value judgement as to which depictions are right or wrong, helpful or unhelpful. What is pivotal here is that these self-made representations were an important part of the way in which the current generation of millennials has conceived of what love can – and does – look like for black people. In his now seminal essay, 'What is the black in black popular culture', cultural studies theorist Stuart Hall argues for "the end of the essential black subject"; a uniform, normative conception of what black people do, what they're interested in and how they love. In this, and other of his works, he argues that a multiplicity of representations allows race (a signifier) to float, invoking different meanings in different contexts. Riveting theory aside, what Hall points to is the communicable relationship between what we see and what we believe is possible for ourselves. Limited horizons of expectation have been tightly bundled into the black experience. With the recent murder of George Floyd, and the worldwide protests that followed, it is understandable why the promise of love may be unfathomable to some of us. And that's why these cultural representations of black love are important. In a world that often doesn't consider, include or celebrate black people, these brief moments of relief, of romance, of love represent more than just a few minutes of fluttery feelings. They represent the ability to dream of a partner who will see you in all your blackness and love you for it. They represent the ability to embrace blackness fully without compromise, and be revered for it. They also represent the potential promise of loving black families, where we are represented in engagement ring catalogues and bridal magazines.

As an adult, my Sunday mornings are the same. I put on the kettle, feed my cats and dig into the Sunday morning Archie - landing on Etta James, Peabo Bryson or Cece Winans. I scroll through Twitter to catch up on the news, drinking a cup of tea. In many ways, black love is about enduring legacy. Our ability to remember, to pass on our gifts, and in a world that seeks to make us small, expand ourselves as we give love and receive love.

Binwe is a Mellon Foundation Media Studies Scholar and internationally-published culture writer based in South Africa.

Binwe Adebayo

 @binwinning

 @BinweA

Malick Sidibé Nuit de Noël (Happy Club), 1963

© *Malick Sidibé Courtesy Galerie MAGNIN-A, Paris*

THE FUTURE OF SEX

EMMA SAYLE

They say you can't reinvent the wheel but you can when most of the world's wheels have been designed by men, for men. You simply rethink the wheel with a female brain and the same can absolutely be said for sex.

Sex has been seen as a simple one dimensional view... a penis in a vagina with the final ejaculation... most of the time the ejaculating is from the male... who knew women could ejaculate too. It's based on perception and stigma — what we've been taught to believe and what everyone instantly pictures when they think about love and sex is a taboo subject that men can high five about and women can blush about or simply remain in silence.

But the future is now a complex web of female brains of every colour and shade and mood combining to reveal a whole universe of sexual options and preferences. As the world of female sexuality, female equality and freedom has opened up so too has the umbrella of sex. What once was a closed door with the simple patriarchal view is now open with an entire spectrum of weird and wonderful levels of pleasure there to explore... and talk about!

Talk! Let's talk about sex! Ask someone in the street where they see 'love' heading over the next 20 years and their feedback will depend mostly on circumstances or visions of how you define love. Why do we blush when we talk about sex? Why isn't it ok to talk about the pleasure you derive from it? Why is it that married women with kids reference sex as a duty to their husband, in most cases to 'keep them interested'. Is it not possible to simply like a good shag now and then? Who doesn't want to escape from the incessant kid demands with a bloody good orgasm.

In short sex has become sexy. Women want to own their sexuality. How that's achieved is a hugely personal journey, but the first step is the approach to the lingo around it. I provide a platform for sex to exist as the 'norm' in peoples' lives; the reasoning behind people coming to Killing Kittens is far reaching but the community and platform are there to remove the judgement and stigma around the subject. Sex is sex... women can enjoy sex, women can talk about it, women can experiment, women can explore (as well as men) and why the heck not discuss it... it's sex and sex for females has become sexy. Our place on this planet no longer exists to 'reproduce', to please the lion pack, we ARE the lioness pack and we're out for meat.

Historically, man and woman 'make love', the woman does her job and makes the man come, the man commends the woman whilst then openly discussing the woman's achievements in the pub with mates. Said woman falls in love, makes babies, opens legs for a weekly bonk in order to stop the man (her husband) wandering. Fast forward to now and beyond... the woman wants a bloody good shag, whether her husband comes or not... The woman points out to the man that his challenge — should he choose to accept it — is to explore the 17 different types of orgasms a woman can have... 17!

We want to provide the freedom for women to explore and experiment in an environment that embodies confidence and ownership. In a female dominated office we openly discuss the latest trends, most commonly searched fetishes and female desires. Those discussions are then made into reality, workshops are tailored to suit a forever growing audience of women ('Kittens' as we call them) who gain in strength and power and frankness. The message is loud and clear — we want to be in control of our pleasure. Whether that pleasure is in pursuit of love is questionable but what is clear is that each and every woman is taking what is often seen as fantasy and turning it into reality.

Should love be happily ever after? Is the path we set out on one-way or can we deviate? Could sex be seen as the freedom to actually create stability within a relationship? Kids/marriage/life, the natural ebbs and flows... all lead to massive great holes in what was seen as happily ever after. But think about this... one or both have a fantasy, it might not involve others, it might involve exploring within the marriage and having sex infront of others. Perhaps it does involve a third party, or more than 3 or perhaps one or both have a fetish they want to explore. Take all those uncertainties that might be leading to friction and a lack of communication embeds itself, leading to resentment and the feeling of being stuck in rut. Chuck in an orgy of 300 people, the excitement of arriving masked and anonymous, the thrill of eyes on your body, the tingle of your nerve endings as clothes are peeled off... if we're going down the romantic route we'd then go along the lines of "my body quivered as my husband's penis entered me from behind as I lay, body entwined with a perfect stranger as I caressed her firm breasts". Or the alternative route:"we had a bloody good fuck in front of perfect strangers, I fiddled with some woman's boobs and then I got taken from behind by some guy whose name I think was Andrew, or was it Roger? Either way I came so hard I couldn't walk the next day." Whatever your approach, by embracing sex, by scaling it back to its basic level of sex being sexy and open to all has the potential to create the stability needed within a relationship that enables its sustainability.

As communication about sex and desire becomes more mainstream, so too does the huge array of subjects that people like to explore. Our most popular workshops involve female orgasms — whilst men ejaculate, women squirt, and squirt hard. Search 'squirting' and you'll be hit with a dictionary of terms, blogs and articles debating whether all women can squirt. Can they? Who cares, the fun is in the trying! Whether it's you trying or your partner trying to make you squirt, it's all about the woman and her orgasm!

Pegging is another hugely popular theme. Hanging your clothes on the washing line? Nope! Pegging involves men being taken from behind by a partner wearing a strap on. Who'd have thought 20 years ago we'd be running workshops on 'How to Peg' with 'pegging' being one of the most widely searched sexual terms. 'Cuckold' has been a historic sexual term — men being humiliated as they are forced to watch their women being taken by someone else. What kind of message is that? A woman being 'shagged' to trigger a feeling of resentment and humiliation in the man. Anyone actually consider the woman might actually enjoy being taken by someone other than her partner?

The world is an open forum in terms of love and the future of love. Over the next 20 years the stage is being set for the ultimate pursuit of happiness and pleasure for both men and women. Will female liberation and the removal of sex being all about the man lead to deeper and purer relationships? Impossible to say. Where subjects were once hushed, buried under the carpet, left as unspoken fantasies and desires, now 'sex' is getting a voice. Terms that were once considered 'filthy' are now mainstream search words, commonplace experiences in bedroom repertoires across the globe. It's impossible to define the future of love but what is possible is to own it, own the lingo, own your bodies and own the ability to be loud and proud of desires and preferences.

Emma is the Founder and CEO of Killing Kittens which organises sexually liberating events across the UK. She is also the co-founder of Safedate and Sistr which both work to empower women and progress their lives.

Emma Sayle

 @emsayle333

 @emsayle

Untitled, 2016.

Alba Hodsall. Courtesy of the artist and Cob Gallery

PLANNING
A FEMME
WEDDING

ALLIE AND SAM CONWAY

Intro: Two women getting married is unfortunately still a pretty untraditional convention, with gay marriage still illegal in many places across the globe. Enter Allie and Sam, a femme lesbian married couple who are rewriting the script when it comes to wedding traditions.

On eloping... it was a last-minute decision for us. Allie was very anxious about the big day, and we didn't want the most important part to be clouded by anxiety forever. It was the best decision we made!

How it felt... it was so low key and relaxed. We had only immediate family there, and there was so much love! It definitely allowed the wedding day to be less stressful.

Saying 'I do' twice... the wedding day felt more like a 'real' wedding than the elopement, so it didn't feel 'fake' at all. It was so cool to get to have both experiences.

Getting engaged... we always knew we'd both propose! Sam thought she'd have to be the first to do it, but I beat her to the punch - which made it that much more of a surprise! I also didn't know when Sam was going to propose back, so it was a surprise for me, too.

Diamond versus gemstone... whoever was in charge of the marketing campaign to convince people they needed diamond rings to prove love deserves a round of applause. We were both just drawn to something different so both of our engagement rings feature morganite and aquamarine.

Planning a wedding as a same-sex couple... we had double the female energy and opinion! But, in terms of how others reacted, we felt very lucky. Every vendor was very accepting!

On choosing a wedding dress... we had two dresses - one for the ceremony and one for the reception. We both designed custom dresses with Anomalie for the ceremony, but had no clue what the other's dress looked like so it was a total surprise!

Seeking approval from parents beforehand... I told Sam's mom I wanted to propose and asked for her blessing! She was so excited!

Did you see each other the night before the wedding? No, we stayed apart!

Walking down the aisle... we both had our mom and dad walk us down. That was so special!

Who gave a speech? Both of us!

Wedding garters... why would any woman ever want their partner going up their dress and removing something with their teeth in front of friends and family... That's weird, right?

Parent's contribution... it's not the olden days and no one needs to pay a dowry for either of us. I know it's nice for parents to contribute, but I don't get why? We're adults right!

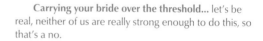

Carrying your bride over the threshold... let's be real, neither of us are really strong enough to do this, so that's a no.

On choosing to adopt... we've both always wanted to adopt! It's also a lot harder for us to start a family as a same-sex couple, so adoption really appeals to us!

How have you found the adoption process? Positive, for the most part! There are always going to be people who like to find issues with things, but we try to ignore them. All our family and friends are very supportive and excited for us which is the most important thing.

Final word? Remember that it is ok to be different. Love who you are and love who you love.

Allie and Sam are a self-described femme couple who are lovers of life, travel & each other. They run a successful blog and Youtube channel together.

Allie and Sam Conway

 @allieandsam

 *@allieandsam_*

LOVE IN THE LYRICS
'SOMETHING STUPID' –
NANCY AND FRANK SINATRA

ORSON FRY

If love between a couple is like a duet, then it's important you learn how to harmonize. Of course there will inevitably be times when your partner (or God Forbid you!) will hit a bum note... but for now let's focus on a great love song which tackles that awkward moment when one of you professes your undying love first.

When Frank Sinatra encouraged his daughter Nancy to take up music again after the breakdown of her marriage in 1965, he couldn't have imagined that two years later they'd be riding the top of the charts with the first ever father-daughter number-one song. 'Somethin' Stupid' was written by Carson Parks, a veteran of the LA folk scene, and first recorded as a duet by he and his wife Gaile. When Sinatra heard the song, he took it to his daughter's producer Lee Hazlewood, the charismatic Oklahoman who had written "These Boots Are Made For Walkin," and they recorded it with Nancy on 1 February 1967.

A clever thing about the song being sung as a duet is we can never be sure who's saying the I Love You bit. Is it him? Her? Who is meant to say it first anyway? I'd like at this stage to ignore the fact that 'Somethin' Stupid' is a romantic song recorded by a father-daughter combo and instead focus on the subject at hand. Being the first to say I Love You can be a nerve-wracking business, and what's more, prove fatal to a blossoming relationship. They were just 'dropping into a quiet little place for a drink' and then Bam, he went and spoiled it by dropping the 'L' word. With no set rules for the language of love, the question of when it's appropriate to say I Love You is one that each couple must answer on their own. All I can do here is recount my own recent experience with using the hallowed phrase.

Unless you've got ulterior motives in love, best to wait until you're quite sure you really love the person before making the big reveal. A good way to be sure that you're sure is to resist the temptation when it first arises—perhaps repeat this a couple of times. Only say it when you really can't help not saying it. With my girlfriend I waited and waited, resisting the urge (perhaps a couple times too many) to the point where she could've been forgiven for wondering if we were even involved in a romantic relationship! Cowardly, in retrospect, I wanted to ensure reciprocation - that my words wouldn't be unwelcome - so I ran it first by a trusty girlfriend of hers. It had reached such a fever pitch after a particularly romantic holiday that it just came out. I whispered it in her ear as we were boarding our separate flights. If you're a last-gasp, slightly paranoid guy like me, airports can be great places for getting things off your chest as you're never quite sure you'll end up in one piece on the other side... But enough of me, listen to the song, and don't let it put you off. I Love You is still the real clincher in a serious relationship—it's just about knowing when to say it.

IN CONVERSATION WITH PANDORA SYKES

PANDORA SYKES

"To be loved is a privilege, to love is a human right"

We are delighted to be in conversation with one of our very first Fenton Friends, Pandora Sykes. Pandora is a celebrated journalist and broadcaster focused on social commentary, culture and lifestyle. In 2017 she co-founded the critically acclaimed podcast, The High Low, along with her friend and co-presenter Dolly Alderton where they discuss current affairs and pop-culture and, in July 2020, she launched Doing It Right, a podcast interview series all about the trivialities, myths and anxieties of modern life. Pandora is also mother to a daughter, Zadie and son, Sasha. She has recently published her debut essay collection 'How Do We Know We're Doing It Right?'

On the books that influenced Pandora's view of love and relationships:

A hugely formative influence in my teenage years was Jilly Cooper; it was how I learned about love and sex, albeit in frequently ridiculous contexts! I learned a lot about relationships, I think, from pop-philosophy, Milan Kundera is a favourite to this day, as is The Course of Love by Alain de Botton. I also love One Day by David Nicholls, which says so much about the subtleties and nuances of the everyday and how you don't have to be in love with someone to have a relationship that is loving.

On the painting that sums up love:

I have a lovely chalk portrait of my daughter and I by Hester Finch, which we made for my husband's birthday. In the end we only sat for five minutes because Zadie had just learnt to crawl so we took a photo and Hester finished the piece after that. It's a very subtle portrait which somehow encompasses everything about our relationship and I can't explain how. It's the wonder of art that it is possible to evoke so much with a single image.

On the physical objects she would pass on to the next generation:

My mother made each of us six leather-bound photo albums of our lives growing up. It was the most generous thing she could have done for four children, holidays and weekends were dedicated to gluing in photos throughout the years. I have my own trove of memories that we were each given at 21 and have of course kept them to this day.

On the advice she would give her daughter about falling in love:

I didn't speak to my parents much about love growing up – I spoke to my older sisters. My main focus is not trying to shape Zadie but guide her. I hope she feels safe and loved enough – with enough conviction in herself – to be her full self, whoever that self is in that moment. After all, the self is not static, it is in a constant state of flux.

When I look back at how I was when I was younger, I am so much more myself now. When I was younger I was so keen to assimilate and make myself palatable. I went to an all girls school where it was important to fit in so I spent and wasted a lot of time acting in a way that was expected of me, or ensured that I would belong, rather than being motivated by anything intrinsic. The sad thing is that this is the age when you are supposed to feel the most free – I wonder, if for many highly-strung teenagers like I was, that's not actually true. I would most like for Zadie to feel free.

On the lessons she would teach her son:

My husband and I already talk about how to raise a feminist boy. I'm lucky that I'm married to one! Something I make a conscious effort to do is not to use adjectives with him that I wouldn't use with his sister. I praise her for being a kind girl, not a good girl. I tell them both they're gorgeous. I wouldn't tell him he's beautiful, so I don't tell her that. It's something I have to actively think about; it's scary how quick the historical social messaging can come out unless you pay attention to it.

When I was growing up there was a clear gender narrative, boys were the naughty ones - the dangerous ones who are coming to take girl's virginity. I think that can be really misleading, boys can feel lonely, confused and emotional in their teenage years as well as girls. I don't want my son to feel like he's a danger, per se, rather I want him to understand that it's his job to make the person he's with – whether that's a man, or a woman – romantically feel safe. In my opinion, love and behaving well are less about the gentlemanly things of paying for a meal, but rather about letting the person you're with take the lead and protecting them, not preventing them.

On a more balanced and open society for the next generation:

When I think about templates for a fairer society, the first thing that comes to mind is the Netflix show, Sex Education. I love that it's relatable but really aspirational in how progressive it is, it's how I hope the world will be in 15 years time. The show doesn't portray the world as it is now, we don't yet have such an open acceptance of relationships, however I would like to think my son and daughters' teenage years will be more like that and have the freedom that the characters enjoy. The depiction of society they've created is very seamless in terms of class and race, it feels optimistic but achievable and is a great social aspiration.

On her hope for progress in the 20s:

An end to violence against women, every time we donate at the High Low we donate to Women's Aid. Over half of UK women who are killed by a man are killed by a partner or an ex and over 75% are killed by someone they know. On a lesser but still important note, I would also like to see more social equality and more nuanced dialogue about childcare – it is not just a woman's domain.

Pandora Sykes

 @pandorasykes

 @PINsykes

Mother and Daughter on purple with pink ground (Pandora & Zadie), 2019 soft pastel on paper.

Hester Finch, c/o Partnership Editions

LOVE IN A
DIGITAL WORLD

GEORGIA LEWIS ANDERSON

I often feel like I'm torn between two worlds. On one hand I consider myself spiritual; I like meditating, am partial to a crystal and sometimes even use a pen to write in a journal. On the other, I'm obsessed with technology and perhaps even naively optimistic about the potential of the technological revolution we're in the midst of to improve all of our lives. I'm lucky to have had a front row seat to some of the most cutting edge developments in the sector in my previous jobs at Google and Microsoft (whilst manifesting abundance during lunchtime, obviously). But what do all these technological advancements mean for the future of our most human endeavour; our love life?

Research suggests 'happiness' (to define the meaning of 'happiness' would be at least another essay so let's take this word at face value for now), can be measured by the strength of our relationships. Let's walk through a broad-brush exploration of this...

To quote the great philosopher RuPaul: "if you can't love yourself, how the hell you gonna love somebody else?!' First, let's consider how technology might change our relationships with who's in the mirror. In an age where therapy is an integral part of an aspirational lifestyle, VR might soon make it accessible for all, and even cheaper than you think, because you won't actually need anyone else to do it. ConVRself are some bright minds in Spain focused on using immersive virtual reality for psychological rehabilitation. Based on the idea that you can always give a friend excellent advice, but it's never quite as easy to find the answers when the dilemma is your own. Their software allows you to see and hear 'yourself' explaining your problems from a third-person perspective. Then you can embody your counselor's avatar (you can choose between a range of famous personalities including Michelle Obama, Steve Jobs or Freud) and respond by giving 'yourself' advice.

I once heard about an artist in New York building her own robot boyfriend and knew I had to interview her for the click-bait title alone. I was intrigued but skeptical; a robot can't spoon you, fuck you or make you laugh when you're upset, I thought. Though what I was left with after our conversation was deeper and more optimistic than I ever could have imagined. Forget the physical, she was building a robot to help her understand what relationships meant to her, that was so personal she even coded it (with permission) using texts from her exs. Soon she spotted patterns in how the data she trained her robot with caused 'him' (he was called Gabriel btw) to react. Leading to her asking herself some revelatory questions about what kind of behaviour she'd put up with in the past, and what she deserved in the future. Now she teaches other women to build their own 'robot boyfriends', often becoming an accidental therapist during the sessions.

We know swiping on dating apps has led to a paradox of choice with the sheer scale of options often proving too much a cognitive load for our monkey brains. Plus there's no way to guarantee that once we've wooed them enough to meet up, that they'll even be a good match anyway.

Dating technology in development instead promises to use search engines infused with AI to find 'hyper-compatible' matches by using data harvested about social backgrounds, sexual preferences, cultural interests, and even celebrity crushes. Some apps already use AI to analyse conversations and encourage users to set-up dates. To ensure you'll actually fancy your boo-to-be on a primal level when you meet, one dating start-up sends users kits to swab their mouths with. Then they analyse the DNA to work out biological compatibility, and combine that with users preferences and backgrounds to unite potential lovers. An example of new-school optimization intended to help people really 'live their best lives.' But do we want someone who's 100% our type on paper? And is it really that easy to turn our personalities and experiences into data?

Let's imagine the methods work and you're in a loving romantic relationship with another human, but find yourselves apart and missing them dearly. VR promises remote social interaction that is more immersive than any other kind of communication. I'm writing this during lock-down so it feels especially prevalent. I think of my friend who's just fallen in love but is unable to hang out with her girlfriend as they both sit tight with their own housemates on opposite sides of the city. Would they benefit from popping on their headsets and being transported to a sea-view restaurant where they could hold virtual hands, look into each other's digital eyes and enjoy the view of a quite real looking ocean?

Scientists believe humans will find emotional satisfaction in virtual encounters like this, in the feeling of sharing a world that just the two of you are logged into where the object of your affection, for all intents and purposes is 'sitting in front of you.' Believing it'll be a better option than even a video call.

Holding virtual hands is all very well, but what about making sweet love? Enter teledildonics; internet connected sex toys (sales of which, incidentally are booming during lockdown from buyers wanting to stay sexually connected). They allow for partners to pleasure each other remotely, with sensations on one end affecting the other.

Technically, there's no reason you couldn't combine teledildonics with a virtual reality world, and who says this world of dreamy pleasure has to be ruled by physics? Why not construct a blissfully psychedelic experience where – for example – one of you touching a 'cloud' causes a vibrator to pleasure your partner. The beautiful thing here could actually be the de-briefs afterwards of what it felt like to have sex in the sky with each others avatars.

We're still in the early stages of course, but I can see how it might be effective, not to mention fun. Interestingly, vision and sound are the easiest senses to replicate. To gaze even further into the future it's re-creating the tastes, touches and smells where the real challenge lies.

So far we've focused on relationships between people, but what about a romantic connection between a human and machine? Romance can mean so many things. If it's comfort, reassurance and loving communication you're after it's not hard to replicate that with a chat-bot. A bot that could run your social media profiles through its algorithm to deduce what kind of memes you find funny and the language you use, and then whatsapp you at sporadic intervals to check-in on how you're doing, offering you encouragement and lols. Sounds like an appealing option in an age of ghosting.

Physical intimacy is harder to engineer, but you've probably heard about sex robots aka the poster-girls for weird tech relationships. I met the man making the most popular models of 'humanoid' machines for customers to have sex with (they need to be rich though, at the time of writing they start at around £5,000) and am open to the argument that they're a helpful tonic for affluent lonely souls who can't foster human sexual relationships for whatever reason. We all have needs, right? An interesting angle to consider are their potential implications for prostitution. Whether you think the relationship between prostitute and client is romantic or not, could robots replace sex-workers? And would the punters be ok with it? It would certainly test the old adage about people only being after 'one thing.' I digress.

It's said the extent to which you grieve correlates to how much love you shared with the one who passed. But what if you didn't have to let that go, and could feel like they were still here with you? If you text someone everyday it's not hard to use an algorithm to keep that digital text correspondence alive. An extreme version of a digital afterlife on the horizon could even be where a loved one could live on using a brain-scan to create a digital duplicate of them. A 'them' that exists in a simulated video game universe complete with all their favourite things, that's able to call you on the phone and Zoom into family chats. How do we feel about the ethics of this? Is it squashing the bereaved from moving on, or is it soothing them? And would our opinions change depending on who the bereaved is? We might feel a product like this is well-suited for a 90 year old man to communicate with his lost wife of 70 years. But a woman in her 30's chatting to a simulation of her dead boyfriend on FaceTime every night might weird us out.

Whilst technology is evolving exponentially faster than humans can ever hope to adapt to, human loneliness and the need for love doesn't seem to be going anywhere. If scientific advances can help people feel less alone, what's the problem? Society has many thoughts about how people should go about loving, but really it's not down to them, or a peer or a religion to make the rules on how or who we should feel affection for.

I often feel that unlike the bulk of human inventions where necessity has been their mother – instead, we kind of have a lot of amazing technological capabilities that we're not actually sure what to do with. We're backward engineering; can we use a computer to be our own therapist? Can DNA swabs and social media analysis lead to the perfect match? Could internet connected dildos and an imaginary virtual world make us feel close to our partner who's on the other side of the world? And if we find ourselves alone, will a machine be sufficient comfort? I'm not sure. Some might feel any impact technology could have on our love lives would be fake, but I'd implore them to consider the very real emotions that develop. Can they be superficial? I guess we'll just have to be inherently human about it; try a lot of things, mess some of them up. And see what sticks.

Georgia is a broadcaster and journalist and former AI personality designer who is exploring her interest in the future of technology in new and unchartered territories.

Georgia Lewis Anderson

 @georgia_la

 @georgia_la

'PROGRESS IS MEASURED BY RICHNESS AND INTENSITY OF EXPERIENCE - BY A WIDER AND DEEPER APPREHENSION OF THE SIGNIFICANCE OF THE HUMAN EXISTENCE'

HERBERT READ

A MATTER
OF HONOUR:
A SURVIVOR'S
ACCOUNT OF
FORCED MARRIAGE

IN CONVERSATION
WITH PAYZEE MAHMOD

Payzee Mahmod is joyful and has a beautiful, confident smile. It's sadly not something that we are always able to say about people who have suffered great tragedy but this is not just a story of heartache and trauma; it is also one of survival and resilience.

Payzee was born in Iraq, her family fled to Iran at an early age where they lived as refugees before coming to the UK when she was 11, where they settled. She told me 'when I arrived in the UK I discovered pop music and I loved reading. I was obsessed with Britney Spears, I couldn't believe that someone like her could be real or that anyone could be so free. I would go to my friend's house because she had a laptop and look at her videos. I loved how she dressed and expressed herself.'

Her family was close. Having fled their country and their culture, Payzee's parents provided the only stability she had ever known and they kept their five daughters closely sheltered. All the sisters had the same long hair and style and were encouraged to obey their parents' instructions carefully. Their traditional Kurdish upbringing was challenged as, in turn, each of the daughters was enrolled in a local school near the family home in South London. Whilst Payzee and her older sister Banaz were still keen to please their parents, their older sister Bekha l– at the time 16 – began to embrace a Western style of life. As she experimented with fashion and new friendships she drifted further and further away from her parents, to the point that she was taken into care by social services.

Looking back, Payzee notes that this marked a turning point in her life; 'It was something that brought huge shame to my family, my father had been a leading figure in our community, someone with great respect who was an organiser of community matters and events. When my sister left, we were shut out by a lot of people because they felt that this showed that my father could not control his own daughters and, as such, had damaged his honour. We didn't speak about it at home, one day there were five of us sisters, and after she left from then on we were four.'

It's the first time Payzee has used the word 'honour' in our interview. Honour is a complex word; it has subtle, sometimes conflicting meanings. There is an association with respect; the Bible encourages us to 'honour thy parents', a use where a woman's honour is used to describe her virginity and a use where honour can denote prestige and power. From this moment onwards, Payzee's fathers' attempts to regain standing and respect or 'honour' in his community were to alter her life and family irreparably.

In order to demonstrate that he still had control of his daughters, Payzee's father began to push them to enter arranged marriages soon after her sister had left. At the time Payzee was only 15 and spending time at home to study for her mock GCSEs. She simply could not believe her father when he raised the topic; 'I only became aware of the idea of love as a teenager from storylines in books and TV, and was hugely sheltered. In most ways I had very little idea of what a romantic relationship was, which was a huge disadvantage because I had no idea what a marriage really was.'

Payzee had always been an eager and able student, a talent her father had previously expressed pride in, however when she said she wanted to focus on her exams he shut Payzee out emotionally in a subtle, yet powerful display of anger. This behavior continued to the extent that Payzee describes that time as a period of 'emotional abandonment'. For a child who had suffered a disjointed upbringing across continents, this was highly traumatic and she struggled to cope with her father's disapproval. So when her mother raised the topic on her father's behalf for the second time, Payzee agreed to be married to a man she had never met.

The man in question was chosen because he had a steady job and spoke English. Payzee's father was keen to give her the impression that this was for her benefit, but in reality this was another move on his part to increase his reputation within the local Kurdish community. First, Payzee was bought in front of an imam to conduct a religious ceremony to marry her; this was then followed up by a ceremony at a local registry office where she was legally married under UK law. She was 16 years old and her husband was exactly double her age at 32.

Payzee recalls; 'throughout the marriage negotiations my parents were very secretive. He seemed more like an uncle to me than a boy my own age. I was trying really hard to please them and didn't speak about it much. I was confused and wasn't really aware of what was happening. When the arrangements were happening I was taken to jewellery and wedding dress shops with both my parents. The owners and sales associates were much more interested in selling things and making money rather than asking if something was wrong. I looked like a child, I was so slim that the smallest size of wedding band wouldn't fit and I was drowned by every wedding dress I tried on, but no one said anything.'

She moved into a home with her new husband and did her best to adapt to the new expectations that were placed upon her to run every aspect of a household whilst still attending sixth form college when her husband permitted her to; 'my friends would go to a shopping center or to eat something after school but my husband would pick me up every day. My friends and teachers never questioned my life at the time, which strikes me as strange now. There were so many moments where someone could have asked what was wrong – my GP, the registrar, a teacher and yet no one cared to do so.'

This is the first time in our interview that Payzee has shown anger; 'it's about children, I was a child and although people may be scared to get involved in a culture that feels foreign, it's the lack of intervention that lets down the most vulnerable people that are part of that culture.' It's very easy to understand Payzee's point when you look at how her sister Banaz was let down by those around her.

Payzee was still married at the point that her elder sister separated from her husband and returned to the family home. It was at this time that she began a new, secret relationship. Payzee's face looks wistful when she talks about her sister; 'she was the embodiment of love in that time. She was starting to think about a family of her own, her boyfriend took her from a dark place and helped her to start becoming the person she was meant to be. I think that seeing her that happy helped me realize that the marriage I was in couldn't be all there was to my love story.'

Banaz's new relationship was seen as a great source of shame to her family who entirely opposed her divorce. This was echoed in the wider community, as rumours of her boyfriend spread she received multiple threats

from cousins, friends and relations. Banaz sought help from the police by lodging five official complaints over a course of several months. She was due to have a further appointment when, with no warning, she disappeared that morning.

Payzee describes that time as a blur, every day she considered a new fate that might have befallen her sister, from having been abducted to 'just being in a park somewhere in the sun'. In a cruel twist of irony, Banaz's disappearance was Payzee's opportunity for escape. She had been lobbying her husband and parents for a divorce for some time, but it was only when the police began to interview her father, uncles and husband that her husband agreed to release her.

Aged 18, after two years of an emotionally and physically abusive marriage, Payzee moved back home, 'it took months for the divorce to happen, the imam was trying to convince me right up until the final moment that I shouldn't go through with it. I walked up and down high streets looking for a lawyer to help me; it took over a year.' It was after she had returned to live at her family home that Payzee learned that her sister had been brutally murdered in a so-called honour killing and that the men who were due to stand charge for her murder included her father and her uncle.

The next years Payzee lived in a state of shock as her father, uncle and their friends were imprisoned. She also knew that without her sister's murder, and the intervention of the police, she would probably not have been allowed to leave her own abusive marriage – 'it was the first time I had seen my husband scared of another power'.

After her father was jailed, history began to repeat itself in the most terrifying manner when she too started to become a victim of community threats and targeting. At this point Payzee left her family home despite her only option beingto move into a YMCA and live homelessly between shelters. She says it was an impossible choice to stay in the community that had cast her sister's death sentence and to live a lonely and fearful life on her own.

'It took time, so much time' but slowly Payzee began to rebuild her life in a new part of London. About six years ago she remembers the first time she felt she had really turned a corner – she was living alone and says 'I started to like doing whatever I wanted! Just simple things like watching whatever I wanted on TV, or spending the whole day in bed without being told off. I had finally found my own safe space.' She now lives in London and has a successful career in fashion. The young girl who was fascinated by Britney Spears' fashion choices now works as an international visual merchandiser and buyer, and is pursuing her own forms of creativity and self-expression. Her biggest career influence remains her mother; 'I learned to sew from watching her and seeing how she could create something out of nothing.'

When I ask Payzee how she feels about her family today she says, 'I still keep in touch with my mother and sisters, but you can't go through trauma like that and have the same relationships you had before. I try the best I can.'

Life is changing, not just for Payzee but also for her entire family; 'When I was 7 I underwent FGM in Iran, I didn't understand what it meant at the time and it was years before I did. I am happy though because of all my sister's daughters, not one of them has or will undergo it too. It's good to see change happening in my own family.'

Payzee's early life has been defined by the toxic search for a misconception of honour that her father undertook and which he valued above the lives and happiness of his own children. In her life, the notion of honour has been totally manipulated and misused to further the true goal of abusive and total control. Payzee sums up the moment her elder sister first left and her father felt dishonoured, 'it's all about controlling women as a way of earning respect. When I was married I was still under the same control my father exerted on me, he and my husband would consult and they acted as a network to exert their authority collectively over the women in their lives.' Banaz's murder was the tragic apogee of this mindset.

But Payzee is keen to point out that this should not define an entire race or culture. 'These bad things don't represent my culture; they are antiquated and harmful practices from across various cultures that need to be abolished. Going to Kurdistan as an adult let me discover it on my own terms, I love the fashion, it's so colorful, I love the food, the old school music, the new school music, the wave of activism, the artists, so many things. I am a British Kurd; my close friends tease me because I drink so much tea. I have some values that are from the UK but there is also a part of my core that is from Kurdistan and it has taught me many of the good lessons of my childhood.'

I leave my conversation with Payzee inspired, emotional and a little enraged. This is the story of a vulnerable child who was groomed, abused and missed part of her education, but somehow all within the boundaries of current UK law. Thanks to her own resilience and strength she has managed to leave this world behind, but there are so many other girls who are – and will be – trapped like her.

I ask Payzee what we can do to stop these practices; 'a huge part of the problem is that we can't even track the numbers – many families will only perform religious ceremonies so the marriage is never officially registered. Even if it is registered, it is still currently legal for a 16-year-old to get married with parental consent. It is this loophole that leaves vulnerable children open to abuse. All forms of child marriage under 18 must be made a crime. People need to speak up when they see this sort of behavior, not turn a blind eye, and the law must support this.'

She knows she was lucky to escape and not suffer the same fate as her sister and today Payzee says; 'I am very glad to say I have experienced real love, the healthy type of love, which is completely opposite to the relationship I was coerced into. I've witnessed father-daughter relationships, which challenge my understanding of those relationships and give me so much hope.'

There is another common use of the word honour. In celebrating and respecting those we love and have loved, we honour the dead. Payzee is now segueing into a full time role as an activist to campaign for change in her sister's name; 'Banaz was so kind and always thought of others. Every day I just want her name to live on and to make it such that anyone who hears her name learns something about how they can help make a difference here.'

HERE'S HOW TO HELP:

Campaign

As the law currently stands, there is no explicit crime of child marriage at any age in the UK. Furthermore in England and Wales a child marriage can be registered from the age of 16 with parental consent, which in reality too often equates to parental coercion. To protect all children from all forms of child marriage (registered, religious and cultural) child marriage under 18 must be made a crime.

Write to your local MP with the following: '@MPName, I am calling on you to #SafeguardFuturesBanChildMarriage to ensure that every child can fulfil their potential.'

Donate

Make a donation to IKWRO – the Iranian and Kurdish Women's Rights Organisation who protect Middle Eastern and Afghan women and girls from child marriage, domestic abuse, 'honour' based violence and FGM (www.ikwro.org.uk).

Payzee Mahmod

 @ikwro

 @IKWRO

'MOST COUNTRIES HAVE UNDERSTOOD THAT WOMEN'S EQUALITY IS A PREREQUISITE FOR DEVELOPMENT'

KOFI ANNAN

HAVING A CHILD
WITH IVF

ALICE MANN

I've never been the type that stopped to coo over babies. In fact as a teenager, I remember saying I wouldn't have children. Perhaps it was because my mother, who'd given up her career to raise me and my sister, never seemed to enjoy parenthood that much, but I couldn't really see the appeal.

And then, of course, I grew up, and found myself in a long-term relationship with a man who wasn't sure he wanted children. Which made me realise that actually I did. When we split up in my mid-20s, I was distraught, but as far as I was concerned, I had years to find a partner, years to become a mother.

But those years flew by, as they have a tendency to, and I was 33 when I met the man I thought I was going to marry, the man I thought was going to father my children. Only he wasn't and after two years, we separated. It wasn't my decision and I spent a year thinking he was going to realise what a terrible mistake he'd made, before I understood that wasn't going to happen.

I spent the weekend after that realisation crying into my duvet, mourning the future we weren't going to have together, but also panicking that, now I was 36, the end of that relationship also meant the end of my opportunities to become a mother. I'd read the articles, I'd seen the stats, I knew my fertility was dwindling, and so I decided to do something about it. I decided to freeze my eggs.

... at a time when everything felt so negative,

I chose to take a positive and proactive step

Freezing my eggs was an opportunity to press pause, to give myself some breathing space. I hoped it would stop me rushing into an unsuitable relationship — "panic buying" as one of my friends referred to it — or becoming one of those desperate daters who see every encounter with a man as an interview with their unborn child's potential father.

It wasn't an easy decision, it was an invasive one — countless self-injections, internal scans and sedated procedures, and an expensive one — £14,000 for three cycles of egg freezing. I joked I'd called my first born Fabergé.

But most of all, it was an emotional one. I hardly told anyone I was doing it — to this day my parents still don't know. And I spent much of the first cycle in tears. It wasn't just hormones, I felt like a failure. I was ashamed I hadn't managed to find a man and have a child the way everyone else had.

Because at that time, hardly anyone was freezing their eggs. If I searched online to see if that strange rash I had was related to the medication, I'd find forums of infantilised women going through IVF talking about "baby dust" and their "DH" (Darling Husband) which made me feel even more alone.

That was when I started eggedonblog.com, a repository for my thoughts and my experiences and the black humour of the situation — one day I walked into the waiting room of my clinic and the radio was playing Ace of Base's "All that she wants (is another baby)" Honestly, you couldn't make that sort of thing up.

The blog is part of the reason I no longer feel shame about freezing my eggs. It became a community that attracted intelligent, successful, like-minded women who didn't want to panic buy. Speaking to them helped change the way I viewed what I was doing and I now feel immensely proud that, at a time when everything felt so negative, I chose to take a positive and proactive step.

Of course, I knew egg freezing came with no guarantees that my eggs would ever make a baby. But at the time I didn't anticipate putting that to the test. They were an insurance policy that I hoped I'd never cash in.

Then I spent three years dating, and despite some maybes (and some unreciprocated yeses, and some who just strung me along), I found myself on the cusp of 40 and still single. And so, reasoning I had a lifetime to find a partner, but a biological deadline to become a mother, I decided to try to have a child on my own.

This had been in the back of my head from the moment I decided to freeze my eggs. I'd even thought about using donor sperm to create embryos to freeze, with a view to going it alone in the future. But my clinic's embryologist advised against it, suggesting eggs would be more useful should I wish to conceive with a future partner.

In the intervening years I'd spent hours mentally going through the practicalities, and the financial aspects, but most of all, the emotional ones. Attending toddlers' birthdays and watching them blow out candles with mum on one side and dad on the other, I'd wonder if I'd always feel that I'd short-changed my hypothetical child by depriving them of that, wondered how they'd feel about never knowing half of their biological family, wondered if I was enough to be both mum and dad.

I still didn't have all the answers but, in December 2016, in those days between Christmas and New Year when most people are eating their body weight in leftovers, and hanging out with their family and friends, I found myself getting to grips with the complexities of sperm donation, and choosing the biological father of my unborn child.

Then it was a simple matter of getting pregnant. Except getting pregnant turned out to be anything but. The first time I tried, they defrosted half of my frozen eggs. Six of the seven thawed successfully, four of the six fertilised correctly, and just one of those embryos was good enough quality to transfer into my body. Still, it only takes one, right? Just not this one. Two weeks later, the pregnancy test was negative.

I'd thought the hard part was going to be making the decision to get pregnant on my own, not the getting pregnant part

Still, I consoled myself, who gets pregnant on their first round of IVF? And so, a few months later, I tried again with the remaining seven eggs. Only I didn't. Because although five of them defrosted successfully, only two of the five fertilised, and both of them fertilised abnormally. This time, there was no embryo to put back. And there were no more eggs.

I was 40 and I'd failed to get pregnant with eggs that were three years younger than me. I was devastated. I felt cheated by the universe. It wasn't supposed to happen like this. I'd thought the hard part was going to be making the decision to get pregnant on my own, not the getting pregnant part.

And yet, for all its apparent futility, I didn't for one moment resent freezing my eggs. I never will. Because the fact that I did it means I never have to wonder whether things would have been different if only I'd frozen my eggs. And that peace of mind has been invaluable.

Because I didn't stop there. I embarked upon another three cycles of IVF using my 40-year-old eggs. The first produced two eggs that both fertilised normally but then they stopped growing: no embryos. The second produced a single egg that fertilised normally, and grew into an embryo that was frozen to use later.

And then things got complicated. Because right after that, I went on holiday with some friends, and I met someone — as the cliché goes — when I was absolutely not expecting to. He was attractive, and funny, and charming, and honest, and emotionally intelligent.

But I had no idea what was going to happen between us, and so I did the only thing I could: I went back to the UK, and did another cycle. That cycle produced an embryo. That embryo didn't result in a pregnancy. And the day I found that out, was the day of our second date. We went for sushi. I drank a lot of wine.

And things progressed. And six weeks after we first met I told him everything. Including the fact that I had a frozen embryo that I wanted to try to get pregnant with. In the next few months. It was quite a bombshell. I don't think I've ever given him the credit that I should have for how he reacted. Somehow, he got it, he understood, he supported me.

In the end, it was academic. That embryo didn't result in a pregnancy either. He was amazing. He could so easily have said the wrong thing. In fact even I didn't know what the right thing to say was, until he said it. He told me there were lots of ways to have a family and we would find the right way for us. And I think that was probably the moment I fell in love with him.

He's continued to be amazing — through a year of us trying to get pregnant the conventional way, through another gruelling and unsuccessful cycle of IVF — his first my, what? Seventh? Eighth, if you count the cancelled ones, ninth or tenth if you count the dummy ones they do to track how your body behaves.

And he was amazing when we sat in front of a consultant who told me, very gently, that based on my history, based on my hormones, based on my age, if we wanted to have a child together, our best chance was using donor eggs.

That was another of those devastating moments.

It would be so easy to feel that the last seven years have been a waste of time, money and energy, when after everything I've been through, I still don't have a child. But I don't. I've done everything I could to become a mother and I don't regret any of it. It's made me the person I am today. It's given me the relationship I have today.

It's the reason why we've signed up with an agency who are trying to find us an egg donor.

That was another of those difficult decisions.

One that's made me reevaluate everything I thought I knew about family, heredity, nature, nurture — and love.

It's been a long story, longer than I could ever have imagined, but it's not over yet...

Some further reading:

Human Fertilisation and Embryology Authority
(hfea.gov.uk)
For independent information about fertility treatments,
and details and statistics from clinics

Donor Conception Network
(dcnetwork.org)
Really useful organisation for anyone thinking about
conceiving with donor sperm or eggs.

**Choosing Single Motherhood: The thinking woman's
guide by Mikki Morrissette\
American but a pretty helpful book to take you
through the things you should be thinking about.

Egged On Blog
(eggedonblog.com)
My blog, my story from start to finish with practical
information, dark humour, sad bits and everything in
between.

The Uterus Monologues
(uterusmonologues.com)
A blog about recurrent miscarriage but also really
good on the emotional side of not being a mother yet.

LOVE IN THE LYRICS
'CAN'T TAKE MY EYES OFF YOU' –
FRANKIE VALLI

ORSON FRY

Bob Gaudio, an original member and principal songwriter of the New Jersey quartet The Four Seasons, called this 1967 classic "the one that almost got away."[5] Gaudio had written the song alongside producer Bob Crewe for Frankie Valli to record, which he did in May of that year. Everyone who heard it loved it, but because it wasn't considered MOR (middle of the road), radio was wary of playing the song. A lot of stations didn't take the chance and it took over a year for people to really hear it. But when they did, it became a smash hit, staying at No. 2 on the Billboard Hot 100 for a week and launching Valli's career as a solo artist.

If any song quite captures the sheer joy of being alive and in love, it's this one. 'Eyes' has all the ingredients of a great love song, mixing equal measures of pleasure and pain. The dreaming and desperate longing of those opening verses, packed into a descending chord structure, suddenly turns and builds with that mischievous horn section to a moment of bold and final declaration. From pining to proclaiming, Valli reveals all his cards in one fell swoop. It's unguarded emotion, straight from the heart and totally infectious. Anyone who's tried their hand at songwriting knows it's easier to write a sad song than a happy one. This song ends up brimming with happiness.

When asked if it was written about anyone in particular, Gaudio responded "It's kind of an amalgam of people and circumstances. Some women, but not one specific, and certain situations that people I've known have found themselves in."[6] Perhaps that explains its universal appeal. It's been covered by over 200 artists across the decades. Andy Williams had a UK hit with it in '68, and Lauryn Hill won a Grammy for her '98 version. Muse covered it, the Killers perfomed it at Glastonbury as late as 2007 and it even became a gay disco anthem when the Boys Town Gang did their own version in the 80's. But for me nothing comes close to Valli's original recording. It's the one that comes

spilling out of the jukebox in the famous bar scene in Michael Cimino's 1978 film The Deer Hunter. De Niro and co. are just about to be shipped off to Vietnam, nothing will ever be the same again; but this song comes on and seems to freeze them in time for that brief moment.

Armed Forces Radio was one station which had the song on rotation during the late 60's, so Valli received a lot of mail from men in uniform. As he saw it, the radio was often the only thing that gave these soldiers the feeling of being home. The words in this song meant something to these soldiers, especially those who had left lovers behind. After the war, some veterans got some money together and hired Valli to put on a show. Only when he arrived at the venue did he discover they had raised the money to hire him by mortgaging their homes. "In a way it was their way of respecting their comrades who had lost their lives," he said; "Vietnam was not a popular war for Americans. The people who came home were spit at and called names and everything else... When they came to give me the cheque, I refused it. I wouldn't take it."[7]

P.S. Beware of any late night attempts at karaoke with this number. Bob Gaudio was in earnest when he said that only Frankie Valli with his exceptional vocal range could have pulled it off. Thankfully the last time I found myself wanting to sing it at a karaoke night, I'd reached such a peak of inebriation as to take myself out of the running. I mistakenly kept writing 'Can't Take My Eyes Off You' next to singer name, and the DJ was pedantic and forgiving enough to skip my turn.

[5] From Bob Gaudio's interview with John Monaghan, Detroit Free Press Special Writer

[6] Interview with BobGaudio - https://www.songfacts.com/blog/interviews/bob-gaudio-of-the-four-seasons

[7] From 'Can't Take My Eyes Off You', Series 17, BBC Radio 4 Soul Music

HOW TO PLAN A GREEN WEDDING

VENETIA LA MANNA

On August 15th 2018, a few hours before we first met, Max went for a run and picked wild flowers. Upon his return to his Peckham AirBnB (he was visiting from the US), he arranged the flowers and wrapped them in a piece of string that he had in his suitcase, placed them in his canvas bag and went on his way to central London where we had arranged to meet for breakfast.

It is the cliché of all clichés, but as soon as our eyes met, I knew. As he placed down the bag, I saw the blooms creeping out, to which I nervously asked:

"How vegan are you?! There are plants coming out of your bag!"

"Actually, these are for you," he responded as he presented the small bouquet.

"I picked them on my run this morning."

My heart landed in my chest. There was something about the attention he had played to choosing, arranging and presenting the flowers. It was understated, resourceful and utterly romantic.

Within ten days, we said "I love you" and then entered into a long-distance relationship. After hours and hours of FaceTime and a few trips back and forth between London and New York, we had met each other's families and close friends and were very much talking about the future. When Max landed back in London for Christmas, we went straight to our local pub for a mulled wine and he excitedly told me he wanted to get married.

One of the (many) reasons why I fell so embarrassingly hard for Max is because of the care he takes over the planet that we live on, being mindful to leave as little trace as he can, and his compassion and kindness towards its people. He also loves a good party.

In June, we set a date for November and started planning our wedding. We knew we wanted it to be intimate, aligned with our green values, and most of all, fun!

The bridesmaids

The bridesmaids wore my old dresses from when I was a little girl which felt so special. I loved how they looked a little miss-matched and it was a great way to save a few pennies, too!

The dress code

As a slow fashion campaigner, I didn't want anyone to feel that they needed to buy something new for our wedding so I came up with the dress code: 'Something Old, Nothing New, Something Borrowed, Something Renewed'. Not only did this mean that there was an incredible array of pre-loved, vintage and rented pieces on the weekend, it also meant that even if our guests hadn't met before, they instantly had something to talk about.

The dress

I opted for a vintage dress that I found in my neighbourhood in London by an incredible designer called Jane Bourvis. Originally two separate pieces of lace, Jane combined the 100+ year old pieces to make the dress of my dreams. I wore it with a pair of dark red second-hand Prada platforms and a slightly ripped veil (steeped in stories), also from Jane Bourvis.

Staying local

Weddings are not all that planet friendly, especially when you're flying in guests from 3,500 miles away, so we decided to host the wedding in the village where my parents live in Gloucestershire, as the majority of our guests were UK based.

One of the best ways we can lower our impact, is to support small and local businesses and this formed the foundations for our special day.

We worked with a local marquee company who ensured that everything we used from the flooring, to the tables, chairs, plates, cutlery and napkins would be re-used time and time again. As it was November, we used a generator to heat the marquee, so if you're keen to lower your footprint, perhaps consider a summer wedding.

FOOD AND DRINK

Food is the third person in our relationship. Max is a chef and I live to eat, so the topic of food was high on our agenda.

Max and I are both vegan (Q: how do you know someone's vegan? A: don't worry, they'll tell you... twice), so we decided that the entire wedding would be plant-based. In order to further support local and small businesses, we worked with a catering company based in Gloucestershire, who were able to source all the ingredients as locally as possible.

After the ceremony, we had (a veganised) english afternoon tea. We of course had tea, and hot mulled wine too to go with stacking platters of crumpets with salted butter and jam, scones, victoria sponge cake, carrot cake and tiny triangle marmite sandwiches.

For dinner, we sat down for a seasonal squash curry for our main and blackberry and apple crumble for dessert.

DRINK

We worked with a local bar company who fashioned a bar out of old barrels. We used as many spirits that were made from waste as possible, one being a sustainable British gin called Boxer, and we swerved champagne in favour of an English prosecco.

We wanted to make the wedding as single-use free as possible, so we went without straws, paper napkins and coasters.

FOODWASTE

We were really careful to only provide the amount of food that we expected to be eaten, but of course, there are usually some scraps and leftovers, so anything we did have was composted in my parents' garden. We opted for doughnuts instead of a traditional wedding cake because in my life, I've never seen a wasted doughnut. And our wedding weekend was no exception.

FLOWERS, PLANTS + DECORATION

In keeping with the little bouquet Max gave me when we first met, all the flowers we used were sourced locally, and the majority from my mum's garden. My mum is a flower fanatic and unearthed the joyful fact that the Aster flower, which grows seasonally in November, is native to Gloucestershire and New England (where Max is from). What's more, it stands for 'everlasting love'. It was interspersed as table decorations, in the bouquets, in bridesmaids' hair and groomsmen's buttonholes.

Our lovely friend Lizzie (Elizabeth Scarlett) is a hugely talented illustrator and came up with some adorable illustrated Aster designs and pileas, which we used on our invites and order of service. We did consider foregoing printed invites and orders of service, but so many of our friends reassured us that they keep them forever as mementos, so we went ahead with them.

Speaking of pileas! We don't have a garden or outdoor space in our London flat, so houseplants are our way of bringing the outside inside and the first present Max bought me was a little pilea from a small plant shop in Richmond. We love Patch Plants (an online plant delivery company) and they very kindly offered us their surplus plants as a way to decorate our marquee, but also to give as presents to our guests to take home. That way they have something to nurture and remember the day by, as our marriage grows too.

For our table place-settings, we collected autumn leaves from the garden and wrote the names directly onto them, holding them in place with little chestnuts.

Even if marriage isn't for you, perhaps you can take away some of these ideas for events or parties you plan. I strongly believe that if we treat the planet and each other with kindness, minimising our impact in small ways where we can, we're in a better position to build long-lasting relationships and enduring love.

Venetia is a slow fashion activist and the founder of the Talking Tastebuds podcast. Alongside her husband Max La Manna, Venetia campaigns for less waste and a stylish, yet sustainable lifestyle.

Venetia La Manna

 @venetialamanna

 @venetialamanna

LOVE

Juno Roche

I was never really sure what love was or could mean to me when I was younger. I remember watching an episode of Sex and the City and honestly believing, despite the heroin I was addicted to, that I could be Carrie Bradshaw and find my own version of Big.

As I sipped my almost-Cosmopolitan (vodka and orange squash) out of a chipped mug, I watched Carrie onscreen and dreamt of being a writer, like her. A writer who would be saved from herself by a man called Big, who pulls up outside her Brownstone and waits for her whilst she changes into a gossamer gown.

I dreamt of being saved from me.

I thought that falling in love would always need a man called Big who would see my fractures and fragility, find them alluring, as Big did with Carrie, and bring love into my life. Then, my version of Big would place his great arms around me, like branches of a gnarled old oak tree, and make a space for me to feel warm, secure, and complete in. My version of Big was paternal and maternal.

I read Mr Big as a protector, rightly or wrongly, that's what I did. I was young and naïve and believed in the only version of love I'd grown up looking at, the one onscreen.

The one that always seemed to be set in sunnier climes.

I looked westwards for love, beyond Notting Hill and Uxbridge, towards California and Hollywood. I watched Richard Burton gave Liz Taylor an impossibly large diamond which became known as the Taylor-Burton diamond, and I dreamt that one day it would be sunnier in my life, and in that sunnier life a man would treat me nicely, buy me a diamond and wait patiently outside for me as I got ready. I thought a man would save me and that, that would be love.

That night as the credits for Sex and The City started to roll, I finished my almost-Cosmopolitan, turned off the television and left my comfortable, exhausted sofa to go out and turn tricks. As I walked out into the balmy East End air I imagined that I was in New York and that I was Carrie. Later that evening when a punter asked if he could kiss me I closed my eyes, ignored his breath, and felt special as his lips encircled mine.

For a moment I was lost.

I was 'dime store Carrie' kissing Big in an alleyway in Whitechapel. I was Carrie, and I was worthy of a kiss. This might be the kiss that saves me; I didn't know if he was my Big or this was my moment, my Martine McCutcheon moment?

As he zipped up and walked away he knew he wasn't the one but I also knew that I believed in love. I always have, despite never really knowing what it was.

When I was growing up there wasn't much love lounging around in our house, although I'm sure there was a lot of love that simply fell into the cracks and crevices around us, wasted because it couldn't be shown, none of us knew how to. Even though we saw it happening on-screen it never permeated into our daily lives. We never learnt how to show or receive love.

I thought that love was a thing that happened after a fight, that someone would hit you and then fall to their knees in tears, and say, 'please don't leave me I love you'.

Me thinking I might be a 'dime store Carrie' was actually the first rung up the ladder towards self-worth. What I saw on-screen I tried to emulate in my quite tricky life, Carrie took me closer to me. I know we can look back now and see the character of Carrie as hugely problematic, perhaps even the whole of SATC, but to me, then, messy as I was, she was light, breezy and optimistic and she always stumbled into appealing versions of love.

When that punter asked if he could kiss me, my lips felt like a pair of butterfly wings that might disintegrate on touch, but they didn't, for the briefest of seconds they melded with his. When we kissed, I was Carrie and he, unknowingly, was Big.

I call myself, 'dime store Carrie' to try and lift the moment into some sunnier Californian narrative, when in truth my life then was essentially grey. That tiny

Americanism, 'dime' allows me to view that part of my history through a lens, not rose tinted but Californian tinted. It's enough. It's not easy looking back and rationalising how you ended up in certain situations or leading a certain kind of life. I never intended to become an addict who earned money in the ways I did.

Being on drugs for years and living that life drained me of almost all joy but then one day, one sunnier day, in some bizarre twist of fate, I found myself flying off to Egypt to see the pyramids with a drug dealer who booked us into the Luxor Hilton and paid for everything with wads of notes.

I felt like Carrie again, despite having been an addict for well over ten years, and thought we'd visit Souks and shop for trinkets.

We never left the room and by day four the drugs ran out. Panic set in.

I, playing at being Carrie again, decided that, in this most surreal of circumstance, I would try to quit drugs whilst sightseeing in Luxor and Cairo.

That was a terrible plan. A truly terrible plan.

I started withdrawing on a sightseeing day trip down the Nile, when I looked up at the sun I felt nothing, not life, not heat, not beauty, just the waves of heroin-nausea washing over me and dragging me down into the tiny space that my upbringing and drug life had afforded me.

I started to violently throw up but Carrie was there right next to me, trying to lift me up and save me; I had to get clean, she would never have ended her days as a washed up junkie on the banks of the Nile.

I remembered the punters kiss in that dirty Whitechapel alleyway and knew that I was worth more than pretending.

I spent the rest of the day throwing up into the small onboard jacuzzi, much to the horror and disgust of the other day trippers out to see the sights. The grey/green me explained to them that I thought I must have food poisoning.

I stared at the flotsam and jetsam that had been expelled from my body, floating on the surface of the jacuzzi, and knew that if I didn't stop now I never would, and that all dreams about versions of Carrie and Big would disappear. If I didn't stop taking drugs I wouldn't have the energy anymore to believe in love.

I got clean by honestly believing that someone like me, a working class trans queer living with HIV, was worthy of love.

I know that 'working class trans queer living with HIV' sounds like a long description but it's who I am, and it's how society tries to consume me, so there is precious little point in trying to build a life based on an enchanting fairytale in which a prince picks out the queer one, the trans queer one, the HIV positive trans queer one, buys them a diamond and whisks them off to a Scottish Croft on the shores of a beautiful Loch.

That was never going to be my life.

I finally understood that in order to become my own version of Carrie that I'd have to let go of her version of Big. Her Big would never save me because I would save me and in doing so I'd start to love myself. I got clean, went to university where I started to write and I didn't stop writing, I never have. I was a writer the whole time that I thought I was just a copy of Carrie, a caricature of her. I thought I was just a caricature of a character who was incapable of understanding love.

Years later I wake up every morning in my small house in the mountains of Andalucía, my pillows plumped up in the middle of my bed and I remember that moment as the turning point in my life, the moment at which I decided that I needed to find out how to love myself a little or maybe a lot, and that if I wanted a gemstone I'd buy my own, a yellow Sapphire set in a narrow band of gold with the words, 'I'll always believe in love', inscribed inside.

No Big, or Carrie, just me: just queer and fabulously contented me.

Juno is a transsexual advocate and campaigner and the autor of 'Queer Sex', 'Trans Power' and 'Gender Explorers'. She identifies as she, her and they.

Juno Roche

 @justjuno1
@JustJuno1

I remembered the punters kiss in
that dirty Whitechapel alleyway
and knew that I was worth more
than pretending

'LOVE IS THE JOY OF THE GOOD, THE WONDER OF THE WISE, THE AMAZEMENT OF THE GODS'

PLATO

LOVE IN THE LYRICS
'CRAZY' – PATSY CLINE

ORSON FRY

Willie Nelson arrived to Nashville in 1960 "as broke as the Ten Commandments"[3] but carrying a suitcase of songs under his arm, that would one day make him a country great. One of these songs was a yearning ballad of lost love which had originally been called 'Stupid.'

One summer night in 1961, Nelson was at the local hangout Tootsie's Orchid Lounge, when he was invited to play one of his own songs on the jukebox. As it happens, Charlie Dick (Patsy Cline's husband) was also in the bar that night and his ears pricked up. He insisted on showing the song to his wife immediately and convinced a reluctant, half-drunk Nelson (it being around midnight) to accompany him to his house. When they got there, Nelson at first refused to go in, but when Cline came out and beckoned, he went in and played her the record. She recorded 'Crazy' the next week.

There is real pain in the singing of 'Crazy' which makes it, in my opinion, Cline's most believable song. Legend has it that when she walked into the studio and nailed the song in one take, she was still on crutches. Earlier that summer Cline had been involved in a head-on collision while out driving with her brother. She was thrown through the windshield, causing her to suffer extensive facial scarring and severe headaches for the rest of her life. At her first try back in the studio, she was forced to abort the session, finding she couldn't sing up to her normal standards. Next time around, Producer Owen Bradley built on this pain and frustration, incorporating her distinctive pauses, elongation of notes and slidings from phrase to phrase to give the song its feeling of real hurt.[4] In doing so he helped Cline to craft the ultimate vocal expression of love lost.

In the 1985 biopic called 'Sweet Dreams' (which despite Jessica Lange's brilliant performance is a flick only for the most die-hard Cline fan), we're led to believe that, in singing the song, Cline was venting her frustration at her abusive, unfaithful husband. But reality paints a picture of a seemingly happy marriage. Without drawing conclusions, it's more likely Cline was accessing one of love's more eternal peculiarities, namely the madness of infatuation. Who hasn't, at one point in their lives, felt crazy in their love? It's a mad and helpless love that Cline is singing about. She knew her lover would leave her for somebody else and break her heart, but she was willing to take that risk anyway. Or rather, she couldn't help but take that risk—love had driven her crazy.

An odd choice for a bridal book no doubt, given it's a song about love lost and not love found; but this ballad deserves a mention as one of the great tributes to this more senseless side of our emotions. Released in October of '61, 'Crazy' would reach No. 2 on the Country Chart and climb to No. 9 on the Billboard Hot 100, becoming one of the first country songs to successfully cross over to the pop charts.

On March 3, 1963, just a year and a half after recording 'Crazy', Cline tragically lost her life when the plane bringing her back from a benefit concert in Kansas City crashed, killing everyone on board. In a strange twist of fate, harkening back to its bar stool beginnings, 'Crazy' has since been named alongside Elvis's 'Hound Dog' as the most played jukebox song of all time.

---

[3] From 'My Life: It's A Long Story', by Willie Nelson
[4] Douglas Gomery in his essay "Crazy" – Patsy Cline (1961), added to the National Registry: 2003

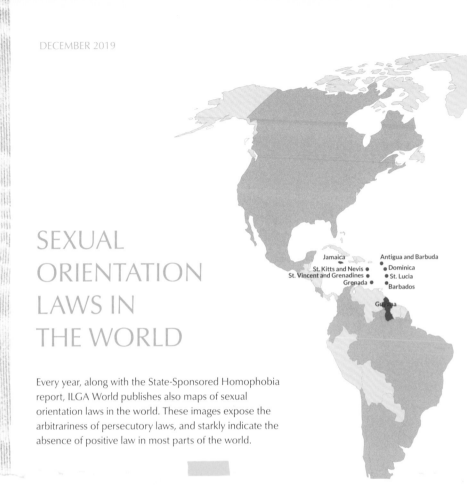

SEXUAL ORIENTATION LAWS IN THE WORLD

Every year, along with the State-Sponsored Homophobia report, ILGA World publishes also maps of sexual orientation laws in the world. These images expose the arbitrariness of persecutory laws, and starkly indicate the absence of positive law in most parts of the world.

Legal recognition of families

Marriage for same-sex couples	23	Other forms of legal union for same-sex couples available*	6

*In Mexico, same-sex marriage is recognised by court order but not all states and municipalities perform it.

Criminalisation of consensual same-sex sexual acts between adults

De Facto Criminalisation	2	Up to 8 Years Imprisonment	30	10 Years to Life in Prison	26	Death Penalty	6 (E) Effective 6 (P) Possible

No recognition of same-sex couples.
In these countries, same-sex couples face daily discrimination

Uzbekistan
Turkmenistan
Syria
Lebanon
Iraq
Iran (E)
Afghanistan (P)
Tunisia
Morocco
Algeria
Libya
Egypt
Kuwait
Saudi Arabia (E)
Qatar
UAE (P)
Pakistan (P)
Bhutan
Taiwan
Mauritania (P)
Senegal
Chad
Sudan (E)
Eritrea
Yemen (E)
Bangladesh
Myanmar
Kiribati
Guinea
Sierra Leone
Ghana
Nigeria (E)
Somalia
Maldives
Sri Lanka
Malaysia
Brunei
Solomon Islands
Liberia
Cameroon
South Sudan
Ethiopia
Singapore
Samoa
Gabon
Uganda
Kenya
Tuvalu
Burundi
Tanzania
Comoros
Papua New Guinea
Cook Islands
Malawi
Zambia
Mauritius
Tonga
Namibia
Zimbabwe
Eswatini

POETRY

MODERN LOVE, DEPTH OF LOVE

LANG LEAV

Love does not grow outward
Like a sapling gently unfurling
It goes inward like the roots of a tree
Piercing deeper and deeper

And when you burrow into this
Dark and desperate place
You find things about yourself
Things about your man
Uncut gems and buried bones

JOY

LETI SALA

If one fine day
your doorbell rings
and it's joy:
spread it and pass it around!
Quickly, to the one
next to you,
as if your hands were on fire!

You're the hostess
but joy is only alive
when shared.

Only when given
will it return to you
maybe in another guise
or shape
      of a flower
            or bounce
                  or word.

THE WEDDING RING SPEAKS

SABRINA BENAIM

sat in the jewellery box   for eighteen years   until her 25th birthday
when her mother   plucked me   a ripe carrot from the garden
cereal box gift wrapped me   & presented me   to her

I rejoiced to return to a finger   even the middle   even on the wrong
hand   I fit perfect   was shameless in refracting light

she loved me   the girl   just as she had as a baby
I was grateful to be a companion again   surprise to find in her
my reflection   two symbols of the same promise

for seven years the girl was faithful to me   only took me off
to bake & then   (of course)   forgets to put me back on
for a few days   but I forgive her absentmind
     the windowsill is better than the dark

having vowed to never marry
     I remain her longest standing commitment
I suppose that means everything works out like it should

this could have been a sad story
     I could have told you about the end   the affair
the girl's own panicked trembling   but none of it matters

when dawn's first light finds me
     on her hand   as it glides cobalt across the page
each morning I sing

          I came from love
          I came from love

& would you believe
     the girl sings along

INDIVIDUALITY, HYMN FOR THE INDIVIDUALS LIKE ME

ISABELLA TOFANI

Hail Mary the lust away
deliver myself from evil
and not into temptation.

She appears to me in a dream.
Red haired devil.
Heavenly. freckles. Glowing skin.
She twists her hair into a grapevine ,
Uses her loose ends
To mark me temptress.

I do not want to stain my Sunday finest
I tell her to wipe off her lipstick
Before kissing me. This way
His blood is the brightest thing
To grace my lips.

Scan Bible study teachings
Is it okay to fall in love with a goddess?

On Sundays
Repent. Confess.
Her breath against my ear
is the holiest feeling.

She moans my name
And a new testament is written.
Repent. Confess.
My hands are reaching for more
than the offering plate.

Walking the garden with Eve
Salivating over her
Forbidden fruit.

Come communion.
When the priest blesses me
Will he be able to smell Yesterday's sin on my breath?
Will he be able to feel her body on my hands?

My bottom lip bleeds corruption
Every time I speak
His name.

Father
Forgive me,
I have been skipping Sunday mass
To sneak her into my Cathedral.

They say to love
Your own gender
Is to become the devil's lover.
Drop to my
knees
And surrender.
I bleed for Him.

Father forgive me
For I have sinned against
Myself.

I sing
To the heavens.
Pull out my ribcage as an offering
Rearrange the Psalms
To look like her palm in mine.
I cannot condemn myself from her touch.

Even the ten commandments
Could not Straighten me out.

I cannot keep singing these Church hymns
If they're going to cleanse her name
From my prayers.

Peace be with those
Who pray for
my redemption.

Though her tender fruit
Slithered its way down my throat
Rotting my insides
I am no longer ashamed.

The only cathedral
I will step into
Is between her legs.

I found eternal life
When I was on my knees
Accepting love greater than any God
I ever prayed to.

I pray
God
If you see me
Breathing the holy Spirit
into her
Do
not
look
away.

ABIGAIL COOK

Passion

Noun

1. a strong and barely controllable emotion.

Origins— from the latin pati meaning to suffer:

I have not seen you in months. If distance is a game, we are both losing: in other words, I miss you.

How to say all of this without cliche?

A friend tells me we use physical pain to describe emotional issues: a stomach dropping, a pull of the heartstrings, a stab in the back. All the things I do to you during that spring. I realise I've made the mistake only after I've made it. That's on me, leaving you, burning down the house we built in our hearts for something better. I don't know what better looks like, I search for it down every dark alley, pick up manhole covers and sift through the sewers.

This is my madness: a ticking clock, a Rizla stuck together by spit, your absence in my bed. Always.

Bear

Verb

2. support; carry the weight of.

Origins— from the latin ferre meaning to **carry**:

I bear the cross of my mistake all through summer and into autumn and winter. I move through the country from the suburbs to a university city to the coast and back again.

I text you. I think you will reply telling me to fuck off, but you don't. You don't say much though.

We fade from one another's lives like an old photograph in the sun. The colour drains from my face and I have a nervous breakdown.

I am lonely, yes, I am so goddamn lonely

I tell the doctor. He prescribes antidepressants and tranquillisers. I sleep through a ghastly January, until Ihave pneumonia from kissing a boy during a play.

The world rests on my chest, and I cannot breathe. I miss you. I miss you. I miss you.

Support

Verb

1. bear all or part of the weight of; hold up.

Origins— from the latin supportare, from sub- **'from below'** and portare **'carry'**.

Two and a half years go by. The fluid in my lungs disappears and I live in a little flat in London. I have dropped out of university twice by this point. And then one day you text me. I am eating croissants from a can, and when my phone vibrates I think it must be a mistake. Your name on my phone, something I have missed without realising.

You say something along the lines of love, except you dance around the actual word. When I reply, I do not. I say I love you when perhaps it would be more appropriate to say I miss you.

I am a good liar but I do not lie to you. You say you might come to England. Every night I lie in bed and think about touching your soft skin. Holding your hand up to my lips. Saying goodnight instead of goodbye.

Six weeks later, you move to London, and into the spare bedroom of my flat.

Hold

Verb

1. grasp, carry, or support with one's arms or hands.

Origins— the noun is partly from Old Norse hald **'hold, support, custody'**.

The first day I hold your hand, is the first day you are in England. We are sitting in the English sunshine amongst trees and the blue sky, sipping on hot chocolate and eating vegetarian curry from the local cafe. I am on the phone, worrying about someone else, when I take your hand into mine. We are friends, that's what I tell myself. Friends can hold hands if they are women.

You will later tell me that's when you realised you had fallen back in love with me. I will tell you, that's when I wanted to tell you all of my secrets, the biggest one being how much my soul had longed for yours. For the years we didn't speak, my soul screamed and cried and yelled like a small child lost in the supermarket.

We go to the supermarket.   We laugh, or more accurately,

giggle.

It is sweet, like bubbles rising in the air.

Sunshine

Noun

1. direct sunlight unbroken by cloud, especially over a comparatively large area.

Origins— could not be found, **but I find it in my lovers eyes.**

The summer of 2019, it is so hot that I dream of opening a window. You are sat at your desk, allowing me to nap even though it is 3pm. A few days later, after we have gotten drunk on gin and tonic's at my mother's birthday, you present me with a ring and say

marry me.

I cry. You bought a wooden box, for the ring, that is etched with our names. I am so overwhelmed I forget to say yes.

But yes, yes, yes.

One year later, we are swimming in the English channel on the hottest summer day of the year so far. We are jumping the waves, and there, in the gap between each one, I look over at your smiling face. Your hair is wet and you are getting tanned.

You glance my way, I smile. You pull me close, and kiss me.

The sea is lapping at our shoulders and all I can think is;

I love you. I love you. I love you.

CELEBRATION

UPILE CHISALA

Bless us for looking inside

Beyond the hurt and the ugliness

Beyond the deep deep tired trauma

Bless us for looking inside and choosing to go in
knowing what we know

Choosing again and again with bone and heart and all
we've ever been to make a home here, a joy here,

a kind thing to hold and celebrate and be true to.

ACCEPTANCE

TAPIWA MUGABE

Thank you for holding my truth with both hands. Another thank you if it is held in the heart with a kind and tender loving prayer.

Dear Ufera,

Love is a wry smile across your face, realising perhaps you knew nothing much of love till you begrudgingly agreed to re-learn and hold again parts of you and the world that had been put away for a good day, a spring day. A day when you could declutter your world, with Love on hand to help you sort out the good bits and burn away the bad ones. Modern love is love as it always has been, perhaps even as it always should have been and you and I my dear are beloved because we get to witness that exists in all its beautiful colours.

Love is a wedding feast. Everybody is present and there is no room for barriers and name calling or putting down under a guise of superiority or inferiority. Coz see, meekness too has its own lessons to learn even after it has saved you. This too shall be something you shall learn to hold in your heart the same way you have learnt to hold anger. The way you carry the first home you come from, how you can only carry it in your heart. The parts that make you shrink in fear and trepidation or sometimes disgust at realising you have lived another man's dream for far too long, forsaking every promise God makes. When you find yourself holding yourself in your hands as something to be afraid of. Accept this too, for power will come from accepting mistakes and re-writing in the tablet of your heart every wrong by asking for forgiveness and accepting that sometimes it won't be handed to you because as we have learnt, our hearts and soul, each ride a different wave and space and time are subject to their laws and we submit to them even in asking for the roses we hand out to be received with grace.

It was a kindness that I poured my beautiful Zimbabwe everywhere and I am besot to know it reached you with grace. This too is a gratitude growing out of the hem of my heart. A little mercy I learnt to say thank you for. Again in words too many my dear I am trying to bestow upon you a new lesson I have recently become a student to. We are all eating at Love's table and learning that our love etiquette will always need refining and adjusting but love itself will never age, never change.

For a while I haven't written to you my Beloved for various reasons however I have decided not to allow fear to govern my mind or my world. And I ask the same of you. Before you accept the destruction that you have witnessed and at times you yourself have caused while in this world, you shall need a vest of bravery to hold all of your delicate parts. I hope you hear it in your bones and in your heart, Love wants all of you without any parts hidden or withheld.

Acceptance starts the moment you sense a discomfort. Comforts are easily acceptable because what's harmful about a safe place. However as an ongoing, flowing river of mind and heart and body acceptance is the place where you sit with time as if in a darkness that lingers too long but never goes away. You will wait for light and at first you may not see it approach but once clarity ensues you will realise you are holding onto the dream of longing for a place to call home. Be it in a country that you have come to call home or in your body, in your mind.

Ufera, when I left Baba's beautiful home; covered in green garden and full of flowers, I left in search of a dream and a half. A backpack and a head full of ideas isn't a best place to start for a child but Ufera, I wanted acceptance into the world, the big grown up world we had all been readied for since learning our abc's and 123's. I wanted to walk into the world not only as an amalgamation of my mother and fathers hard work or my own fancies but also as a man who knows a chance at life is all the chance we ever need to live and live abundantly so. At first I found no place that could hold a black boy with butterfly wings. Years of living in a place that refuses you has left me painting walls and nailing permanent fixtures to the walls of my impermanent abode. You see the acceptance we give others is often the acceptance we long for. And if you have time to understand this you will learn how the acceptance we long for is often what we need to give others. So I hope you find this letter full of all the things lovers forget to say in-between kisses and before a blush blossoms into an emotion with a name you can put a face to.

That slow drop of love from a foreign place that feels familiar. That memory of home that you haven't seen for a while but smells like yesterday the moment you see it. Acceptance is the punch your brother gives you when you find him gathering roses into his big man chest only to end up telling you, you sound like you need a chat. We long for home and homes in places where we try to make ourselves a home without invitation too. Chasing that ever elusive peace by that prevails over us and our world (everything) when we come to a place where we can hold our truth with both hands.

Our truth that our blue and green marble which we call home needs better looking after. Accepting that our home, Earth, before we find other places to habitat needs a lifetime of tenderness. That we want to leave a place full of roses and bees in our gardens and all the green of this world so our future generations can also give roses and receive them as a gift of love and joy. Accepting that there are times when our leaders are human beings with flaws and that all the money in any value in the world is never enough to equate to any human being.

To hold truth with both hands is to accept that there will always be two truths to any narrative told by humans and with those truths are falsehoods that when accepted as we accept truth, with love and freedom, perhaps a clearer truth is seen. Having searched for truth, at a time when it has become distorted I found myself accepting that a world without God is another that never ends and a flood I never want to glimpse even from afar. So I accepted that all the wonders and laws of our universe are held in perfect repose under the world archduke eye of our Maker. And it is in His rest that I found a beautiful place to hold all of my truths. And as for being an alien, I belong to God and in the church I found a place to belong, accepted with a modern love that sounds a lot like Jesus.

Read:

Psalm 139:14

I praise you because I am fearfully and wonderfully made; your works are wonderful, I know that full well.

Lastly, I ask that you continue to work. Work at your heart, work on your mind and work with your body. This is the only way to accept that this life though burdensome and weary, is full of roses at every turn when we wake up in faith to do that which we love with love and will (iva neChido neRudo).

All of my love, always and forever

Tapiwa Mugabe.

'I'm for truth,
no matter who tells it.
I'm for justice,
no matter who it is
for or against'

Malcolm X

OUR CHARITIES

Our contributors chose:

Black Minds Matter

Black Minds Matter's mission is to be part of making mental health topics relevant and accessible for all black people in the UK. They have put together a support network and organisation to enable as many black people as possible to get specialised mental health support. They do so by connecting black individuals and families with professional mental health services across the UK and funding their treatment.

www.blackmindsmatteruk.com

The Albert Kennedy Trust (AKT)

AKT supports LGBTQ+ young people aged 16-25 in the UK who are facing or experiencing homelessness or living in a hostile environment. The trust supports young people into safe homes and employment, education or training, in a welcoming and open environment that celebrates LGBTQ+ identities.

www.akt.org.uk

women's aid
until women & children are safe

Women's Aid

Women's Aid is at the forefront of shaping and coordinating responses to domestic abuse. Their work encompasses a broad range of activities ranging from helping survivors and supporting their members to campaigning for legal change and launching programs for research and education. Each year, they help thousands of women escape abuse and rebuild their lives.

www.womensaid.org.uk

The Fenton Team chose:

IKWRO

IKWRO was founded as the Iranian and Kurdish Women's Rights Organisation in 2002. IKWRO's mission is to protect Middle Eastern and Afghan women and girls who are at risk of 'honour' based violence, forced marriage, child marriage, female genital mutilation and domestic violence and to promote their rights. They provide direct services for women and girls, including advocacy, training and counselling.

www.ikwro.org.uk

Alexandra Shulman chose:

Coram Beanstalk

Coram Beanstalk recruits, trains and supports volunteers to provide one-to-one literacy support in early years settings and primary schools to children who have fallen behind with their reading. Their aim is that Coram Beanstalk will be supporting 20,000 children every year by 2020-21, providing them with the one-to-one reading support they need to thrive in life.

www.beanstalkcharity.org.uk

IMAGE ACCREDITATIONS

What is Love? p2 - *Nude on grey with red shadow & blue plant* © Hester Finch, c/o Partnership Editions

Iconic couples pg 37 - *Oscar Wilde, photographic print* © This work is in the public domain in its country of origin and other countries and areas where the copyright term is the author's life plus 100 years or fewer."

Brides who went their own way p23 - *Lydia Pang Wedding Dress* © Victoria Somerset-How Photography

Gerda Wegener portrait of Lili Elbe p38 - *Portait of Lili Elbe* © Gerda Wegener died in 1940, so this work is in the public domain in its country of origin and other countries and areas where the copyright term is the author's life plus 75 years or fewer.

Brides who went their own way p24 - *Poppy wedding dress* © Photograph courtesay of Gianluca Longo

Bob Dylan - Love in the Lyrics p45 - *Bob Dylan* © Bob Dylan, August 28, 1963. By Rowland Scherman - This media is available in the holdings of the National Archives and Records Administration, cataloged under the National Archives Identifier (NAID) 542021, Public Domain

George Harrison - Love in the Lyrics p30 - *George* © This file is made available under the Creative Commons CC0 1.0 Universal Public Domain Dedication.

Why you shouldn't lose your virginity p66 - *Nude on grey with white blanket & blue wall* © Hester Finch, c/o Partnership Editions

Smokey Robinson - Love in the Lyrics p91 - *Trade ad for Smokey Robinson & the Miracles's single "Going To A Go-Go"* © This image from an advertisement is in the public domain

The future of Sex p132 - *Untitled, 2016* © Alba Hodsall. Courtesy of the artist and Cob Gallery

Patti Smith - Love in the Lyrics p103 - *Patti Smith* © Patti Smith performing at Cornell University, 1978 - Vistawhite. This file is licensed under the Creative Commons Attribution 3.0 Generic license.

Frank and Nancy Sinatra p141 - Love the pyrics - *Photo of Frank and Nancy Sinatra performing on the 1966 television special* © Image in the public domain

Nick Cave - Love in the Lyrics p114 - *Nick Cave* © Futurama - Deinze - Belgium - 1986 - Yves Lorson. This file is licensed under the Creative Commons Attribution 2.0 Generic license.

In conversation with Pandora Sykes p142 - *Mother and Daughter on purple with pink ground (Pandora & Zadie), 2019 soft pastel on paper*© Hester Finch, c/o Partnership Editions

Black Love Story p128 - *Nuit de Noël* © Malick Sidibé, Nuit de Noël (Happy Club), 1963 © Malick Sidibé. Courtesy Galerie MAGNIN-A, Paris

Pasty Cline - Love in the Lyrics p181 - *Patsy Cline promotional photo from March 1957 - Author: Four Star Records.* © Image in the public domain

ACKNOWLEDGMENTS

Clara Dessaint and Aisle8   Copyediting

Lucy Dawn Bayliss   Art Direction and Illustrations

CPI   Design

All our contributors

Abigail Cook	Isabella Tofani
Alain de Botton	Juno Roche
Alexandra Shulman	Kate Wills
Alice Mann	Lang Leav
Allie and Sam Conway	Leti Sala
Binwe Adebayo	Luke Day
Candice Brathwaite	Olivia Petter
Clement Knox	Orson Fry
Dr Sophie Mort	Pandora Sykes
Edward Downpatrick	Payzee Mahmod
Elizabeth Day	Polly Vernon
Em Clarkson	Sabrina Benaim
Emily Yates	Sarah Royce-Greensill
Emma Sayle	Sharmadean Reid MBE
Flora Gill	Tapiwa Mugabe
Georgia Lewis Anderson	Upile Chisala
Gianluca Longo	Venetia LaManna
Holly Bourne	Vick Hope

ILGA   The sexual orientation laws in the world map is supported by the data collected in State-Sponsored Homophobia 2019: Global Legislation Overview Update (published in December 2019) and incorporates some of the legal developments that took place since then, including civil partnerships in Monaco, marriage equality in Costa Rica, and the unfortunate repeal of the antidiscrimination law in North Macedonia.